CRACKS IN THE FOUNDATION: DEALING WITH DOUBT

Ivette Smith

COPYRIGHT

TABLE OF CONTENTS

COPYRIGHT ii

INTRODUCTION vii

CHAPTER 1 UNDERSTANDING FAITH AND DOUBT 1

1.1 The Anatomy of Faith: Beyond Belief 1

1.2 The Anatomy of Faith: Delineating Its Components and Process.... 5

1.3 Faith as a Dynamic Journey: An Evolving Process 7

1.4 Faith in Various Contexts: Manifestations Across Religions and Spiritual Practices 8

1.5 Doubt as a Positive Force: A Pathway to Growth 11

1.6 The Role of Doubt in Faith Development 12

1.7 Cultural and Historical Influences on Belief Systems 17

1.8 Strategies for Embracing Doubt 18

5. Embracing Doubt as a Path to Growth 19

1.9 Cultural Influences on Faith: Shaping Beliefs Across Contexts 19

1.10 Historical Shifts in Belief Systems: How Events Shape Faith Narratives 21

1.11 The Interplay Between Culture and Doubt: Suppression and Encouragement 23

1.12 The Impact of Globalization: Interconnectedness and the Evolution of Belief Systems 24

1.13 The Dynamic Relationship Between Culture, History, and Faith 25

CHAPTER 2 THE EMOTIONAL LANDSCAPE OF FAITH TRANSITIONS 27

2.1 The Emotional Highs and Lows: Intense Reactions to Questioning Faith 27

2.2 Common Emotional Experiences in Faith Transition 28

2.3 The Psychological Impact: How Emotional Turmoil Affects Mental Health 31

2.4 Coping Strategies: Practical Advice for Managing Emotional Turmoil..32

2.5 Personal Narratives of Faith and Doubt 34

1. A Tale of Two Beliefs: From Faithful to Skeptic....................34

2. Highlighting Key Turning Points: Shifting from Belief to Skepticism 36

3. The Emotional and Intellectual Struggles of Transition...................37

2.6 Resolutions and Outcomes: Finding a New Sense of Understanding 38

2.7 Rediscovering Belief After Crisis 39

The Deconstruction Process: Unraveling and Rebuilding Beliefs........40

1. Illustrating the Deconstruction Journey...................................40

2. Examining Catalysts for Deconstruction..................................41

3. The Rebuilding Phase: Reconstructing Beliefs Post-Deconstruction..42

4. Challenges and Revelations During the Deconstruction and Reconstruction Phases..44

The Deconstruction Process as a Path to Rebirth 45

CHAPTER 3 LEAVING RELIGION: STORIES OF SPIRITUAL INDEPENDENCE...46

1. Narrating Experiences of Leaving Organized Religion....................46

2. Discussing Reasons for Leaving Organized Religion 47

3. Examining the Challenges of Leaving Religion...............................48

4. Highlighting the Benefits of Spiritual Independence 49

The Path of Spiritual Independence 51

1. Defining Your Spiritual Identity: Beyond Labels 51

2. Creating Sacred Spaces: Personal and Communal Practices............52

3. Incorporating Diverse Beliefs: A Holistic Approach 53

4. Embracing Spiritual Flexibility: Adapting Beliefs Over Time.........53

5. Defining Your Spiritual Identity: Beyond Labels 55

6. Identifying Influences: Recognizing the Impact of Past Experiences on Current Beliefs 56

7. Discussing the Limitations of Traditional Labels: Moving Beyond Binary Classifications 57

8. Crafting a Personal Spiritual Narrative: Telling Your Own Story ...58

9. Highlighting the Value of a Flexible Spiritual Identity 59

2. Spiritual Autobiography 61

3. Belief Audit 62

4. Writing a Spiritual Mission Statement 63

5. Guided Meditation: Exploring Spiritual Identity 64

6. Letting Go with Gratitude 65

CHAPTER 4 PHILOSOPHICAL AND INTELLECTUAL EXPLORATION: MORAL DILEMMAS WITHIN FAITH 67

4.1 The Complexity of Moral Decision-Making 67

4.2 Philosophical Debates on Divine Existence 70

4.3 Exploring Secular Ethics and Spiritual Morality 71

CHAPTER 5 PRACTICAL GUIDANCE FOR NAVIGATING DOUBT 73

5.1 Mindfulness Practices: Grounding the Spirit 75

5.2 Engaging in Open Dialogue: Conversations That Heal.................77

5.3 Seeking Reliable Guidance: Identifying Trustworthy Sources 79

CHAPTER 6 EMPATHY AND UNDERSTANDING IN FAITH DISCUSSIONS 82

6.1 Respecting Differences: Building Interfaith Bridges 84

6.2 The Power of Storytelling: Sharing and Receiving Faith Narratives 86

6.3 Healing Divides: Creating Inclusive Spiritual Spaces...................88

6.4 LGBTQ+ Perspectives: Faith and Identity 92

6.5 Technology and Spirituality: The Digital Faith Frontier...............94

6.6 Environmental Stewardship: Faith-Based Activism 96

CHAPTER 7 OVERCOMING FEAR AND JUDGMENT.....................99

7.1 Inner Critic: Overcoming Self-Doubt and Fear............................101

7.2 Finding Strength in Vulnerability: Embracing Authenticity 103

7.3 Transforming Fear into Courage: The Path to Empowerment 104

CHAPTER 8 INSPIRATIONAL AND MOTIVATIONAL CONTENT 107

8.1 Inspirational Figures: Learning from Spiritual Guides.................109

8.2 Motivational Messages: Finding Hope Amidst Doubt 111

8.3 Embracing the Journey: Finding Joy in Exploration 113

CHAPTER 9 PRACTICAL SOLUTIONS FOR FAITH INTEGRATION 116

9.1 Faith in Action: Living Beliefs Through Service 118

9.2 Navigating Faith in Relationships: Building Supportive Bonds...120

9.3 Balancing Faith with Career: Maintaining Spiritual Integrity 122

CHAPTER 10 THE FUTURE OF FAITH AND DOUBT...................125

10.1 Envisioning a Personal Spiritual Future: Setting Intentions.......127

10.2 The Role of Faith in a Changing World: Adapting to New Realities 129

10.3 Embracing Mystery: The Beauty of Unanswered Questions......131

FAITH OR SELF-HELP? 134

CONCLUSION 138

REFERENCES 140

INTRODUCTION

Years ago, I found myself on a cold bench outside a church, feeling the weight of the universe pressing down on me. I had attended a service, hoping for clarity, but instead, I was left with a heart full of questions. I remember looking up at the vast sky, the stars winking like distant promises, and wondering where I truly belonged. It was a moment of profound doubt, one that many of us have felt when our faith seems to falter and the world grows silent.

This book is born from such moments of doubt, confusion, and transition. It aims to explore the journey through faith and uncertainty, highlighting that these experiences are not only common but often lead to personal growth. Don't get me wrong. This is not a self-help book. It is a series of suggestions to expand awareness of the world within you. A lot of people know much about spiritual ideas and beliefs, yet only some really know what it feels like to be connected to their spiritual essence in daily life. We all face times when our beliefs are challenged, when the foundation we once stood on begins to crack, and we no longer feel connected to that spiritual essence. These instances shape us, urging us to search deeper and understand more fully.

What sets this book apart is its unique blend of personal stories, philosophical insights, and practical advice. It's not just about recounting tales of spiritual struggle; it's about offering a companion through the labyrinth of questions and the potential answers that follow. Here, you'll find narratives that resonate with your own experiences, reflections that provoke thought, and guidance that helps navigate the journey.

This book is intended for adults and young adults who find themselves questioning their spiritual identity, grappling with doubt, or searching for meaning. You might be moving between religious beliefs, stepping away from organized faith, or simply yearning for understanding. Whatever your path, you are not alone. Many share these struggles, and we can find comfort and connection through shared stories.

The book is structured to guide you through various stages of this journey. Each chapter focuses on different themes: personal narratives that anchor you in authentic experiences, intellectual challenges that stimulate your thinking, and practical guidance that offers a way forward. These elements work together to provide a comprehensive exploration of faith and doubt.

Central to this book is the importance of open dialogue. We need spaces where questions are welcomed, where differing perspectives are understood, and where empathy reigns. This book encourages such conversations, aiming to bridge gaps and foster understanding among diverse beliefs.

In today's world, faith and doubt are influenced by many factors. Secularism is rising, interfaith interactions are more common, and technology is reshaping spirituality. These trends create a complex landscape where beliefs are constantly evolving. This book sets these changes in context, helping you navigate your path amidst these shifts.

As you read, I invite you to reflect on your own spiritual journey. Consider how the themes in this book resonate with your experiences. Engage with the content actively, allowing it to challenge and inspire you.

This exploration is backed by extensive research from psychology, theology, and personal interviews. These sources provide a well-rounded view, ensuring the book is credible and insightful.

As we conclude this introduction, let me leave you with a note of hope. This book is an invitation to a journey of self-discovery and spiritual growth. It's a chance to embrace your doubts, honor your questions, and find more profound truths. May it inspire you to continue seeking, finding solace in the knowledge that every path, no matter how uncertain, holds the promise of light.

CHAPTER 1

UNDERSTANDING FAITH
AND DOUBT

There was a time when I stood on the edge of a cliff, not literally, but in the realm of belief. It was an ordinary day, yet the ordinary often masks the profound. The sun was setting, casting long shadows that seemed to reach into the very depths of my being. I was caught between the certainty of science, the tangible, and the whispers of faith, the unseen. This moment, where faith and doubt collided, was cathartic. It taught me that faith is not a monolith but a tapestry woven with threads of trust, emotional commitment, and the stories we tell ourselves. As you read this chapter, consider your own moments of standing on the precipice, questioning, and seeking.

1.1 The Anatomy of Faith: Beyond Belief

Faith, while often equated with belief, is far more intricate and layered. It's not just the intellectual acceptance of a set of doctrines but a more profound, multidimensional experience that involves trust, emotional investment, and a sense of commitment. To truly understand faith, we must break it down into its core components, each adding depth to the concept of belief. This examination will reveal that faith goes beyond simply "believing" in something—it encompasses trust, confidence, emotional commitment, and a lived expression that permeates one's entire being.

Faith is not static; it evolves over time. Just as we grow and change, so too does our faith. According to James W. Fowler's faith development theory, individuals move through various stages, beginning with childhood beliefs and progressing to a more complex spiritual understanding in adulthood. This evolution is influenced by life experiences, which act as catalysts for deeper reflection and transformation. Significant events, whether joyous or challenging, are major events that often prompt us to reassess our beliefs, leading to growth and a more nuanced spirituality. This process is dynamic, a continual unfolding rather than a destination.

Belief as the Starting Point

Belief is the cognitive foundation of faith—it represents the intellectual aspect where a person holds specific ideas or propositions to be true. For many, this is the entry point into faith: accepting a higher power, a moral framework, or a set of religious teachings. However, belief alone is often fragile. It can be challenged by reason, doubt, or external circumstances. Without more resounding support, belief can waver when confronted with adversity.

Faith manifests in diverse ways across different religions and spiritual practices. In monotheistic religions, faith often revolves around a singular divine entity, emphasizing a personal relationship with God. This personal connection is central, providing a direct line to the divine. In contrast, polytheistic religions may focus on a pantheon of deities, each representing different aspects of life and the universe. Here, faith is expressed through a tapestry of stories and rituals that honor the complexity of existence. Spirituality without organized religion, too, has its place, offering a path for those who seek connection with the divine outside traditional structures. This form of spirituality emphasizes personal experience and inner exploration, allowing for a fluid and individualized expression of faith.

Trust: The Relational Aspect of Faith

Trust goes beyond belief. It is an act of placing one's confidence in something or someone, even when evidence or certainty is lacking. While belief might focus on the "what," trust focuses on the "who"—the relationship between the believer and the object of their faith. Whether it's trusting in a deity, the universe, or the inherent goodness of life, this aspect of faith implies a willingness to lean on something larger than oneself. Trust enables people to hold onto their faith during times of doubt or confusion, even when they cannot fully explain or understand their beliefs.

For example, someone may intellectually believe in the concept of a loving God. Still, trust enables them to rely on that love during personal crises despite not having direct proof of it. Trust in faith is often tied to vulnerability, which requires letting go of control and accepting uncertainty.

Confidence: The Assurance that Fuels Faith

Confidence is the certainty that grows from both belief and trust. It's not just the belief that something is true or that a relationship exists—it's the sense of security that comes from past experiences of faith being justified. Confidence in faith develops over time through lived experiences, moments of spiritual fulfillment, or answers to prayer that reinforce the individual's trust. It's this confidence that helps to strengthen faith when it's under attack by external or internal doubts.

While trust requires vulnerability, confidence offers reassurance. It serves as the emotional armor that allows believers to withstand challenges. Faith is often tested through hardship, and confidence provides the resilience necessary to keep going. In moments of crisis, confidence can anchor faith, reminding believers of the times their trust was met with validation.

Emotional Commitment: The Heart of Faith

While belief and trust are essential, faith ultimately becomes meaningful through emotional commitment. This is where faith transcends intellectual acknowledgment and enters the realm of personal identity and purpose. Emotional commitment to faith manifests as a deep, passionate investment in one's beliefs—shaping decisions, behavior, and one's approach to life itself.

This emotional dimension is what makes faith feel so personal. It is what brings fervor to religious devotion or drives individuals to defend their faith against opposition. Emotional commitment also explains why faith is often resilient despite logical contradictions. It's not merely about "knowing" something to be accurate but "feeling" connected to it in a way that shapes the core of one's being.

For example, a person might remain emotionally committed to their faith community even after they experience doubt about its teachings because it offers them a sense of belonging, purpose, and emotional fulfillment. The commitment to community or ritual can be just as sustaining as intellectual belief.

Faith as a Lived Experience

Finally, faith is not just something people hold; it's something they live. It moves beyond belief and enters the everyday reality of actions, choices, and interactions. Faith influences moral decisions, inspires acts of compassion, and provides comfort in times of grief or uncertainty. It's a guiding force that informs how people navigate life's challenges and joys. People often cling to this faith when their intellectual belief is challenged, as their identity and community are intertwined with their faith experience.

Faith that is lived out creates habits and rituals, reinforcing trust, confidence, and emotional commitment. These practices—whether prayer, meditation, communal worship, or service—become ways to actively engage with and express faith.

Faith is far more than a set of beliefs or doctrines—it's a complex, dynamic force that touches every aspect of life. It involves trust, confidence, and emotional commitment, all working together to form a deep connection between the individual and their spirituality or philosophy. Faith is not just about intellectually agreeing with ideas; it's about trusting in something exceptional, committing emotionally to that trust, and living out that commitment in a meaningful way.

In this way, faith is a lived experience, not just a cognitive one, and it endures through life's complexities, uncertainties, and emotional depths. Understanding faith in this holistically allows us to see its power to transform lives, give meaning, and sustain hope.

1.2 The Anatomy of Faith: Delineating Its Components and Process

Faith is a deeply personal and multifaceted experience that shapes individuals' perceptions of the world, their sense of purpose, and their connection to something greater. However, faith cannot be reduced to belief alone—it involves cognitive, emotional, and social elements. Additionally, faith is not a static state but an evolving journey shaped by life experiences and personal growth. Below, we break down the various components and dimensions of faith, exploring how it manifests across different religions and secular contexts.

Components of Faith: Cognitive, Emotional, and Social Elements

Cognitive Faith: Beliefs and Doctrines as Mental Frameworks

Cognitive faith refers to the intellectual component of belief. It involves the acceptance of specific doctrines, theological principles, or religious teachings that form the mental framework for an individual's faith. These beliefs might include concepts of God, moral imperatives, or spiritual truths.

- Doctrines and Dogmas: Cognitive faith often begins with accepting key tenets specific to a religion or philosophy. For example, monotheistic faiths like Christianity, Judaism, and Islam revolve around the belief in one God, whereas polytheistic traditions such as Hinduism have multiple deities with varying roles.

- Worldview Shaping: These mental frameworks help believers make sense of the world, explaining life's mysteries, morality, and existence. Cognitive faith allows individuals to process and integrate their beliefs intellectually.

Emotional Faith: The Role of Feelings and Experiences in Sustaining Belief

Emotional faith is the affective, experiential side of faith. It refers to the emotions, personal experiences, and inner transformations that sustain and nurture belief.

- Emotional Resonance: Faith often involves a deep emotional connection, whether it's the joy of feeling adivine presence, the comfort in moments of prayer, or the peace from surrendering to a higher power. These emotions reinforce cognitive beliefs, making faith feel more personal and real.

- Spiritual Experiences: Moments of transcendence, awe, or divine encounter can profoundly shape emotional faith. Whether it's a conversion experience, a sense of purpose, or moments of peace in times of crisis, emotional experiences help individuals stay connected to their faith even when intellectual doubts arise.

Social Dimensions: Community and Tradition as Pillars of Faith

The social aspect of faith is often its most visible dimension, rooted in shared rituals, communal worship, and tradition.

- Community Belonging: Faith is often sustained by being part of a community of believers. This communal aspect provides support, accountability, and a sense of identity as people share in rituals, collective prayer, and festivals. Religious traditions like weekly worship services, celebrations, or pilgrimages reinforce social bonds and sustain faith through shared experiences.

- Transmission of Faith: Tradition is crucial in maintaining faith across generations. Through socialization within families and religious institutions, individuals learn their faith's practices, stories, and teachings. This process of enculturation helps maintain continuity and identity within faith communities.

1.3 Faith as a Dynamic Journey: An Evolving Process

As I've said before, faith is not a static, unchanging state but an evolving journey. As individuals grow and experience life, their faith changes, matures, and transforms in response to new insights and challenges.

Faith Development Stages: From Childhood Beliefs to Adult Spirituality

Faith often begins with simple, concrete ideas during childhood but evolves into a more complex, nuanced understanding in adulthood.

- Childhood Faith: Faith is often simplistic and rule-based in early stages of life, faith is often simplistic and rule-based, tied to familial or cultural traditions. Children tend to adopt their parents' and communities' beliefs and practices, frequently viewing faith in black-and-white terms—right vs. wrong, good vs. evil.

- Adolescent Questioning: As individuals enter adolescence, they begin to question these beliefs, exploring doubts and contradictions. This stage often involves a period of wrestling with faith, searching for answers, and forming a personal spiritual identity.

- Adult Spirituality: In adulthood, faith becomes more reflective and personal. It may integrate doubt and ambiguity, moving from a rigid adherence to doctrines to a more open, fluid relationship with spirituality. Adult spirituality often embraces paradox, mystery, and a more profound sense of purpose.

The Impact of Life Experiences: How Major Events Shape Faith

Life events such as loss, trauma, or joy can significantly reshape an individual's faith.

- Crisis of Faith: For some, tragedy or loss may trigger a crisis of faith, causing them to question long-held beliefs. Conversely, moments of grace or healing may reaffirm one's belief in a higher power. These experiences act as catalysts for faith transformation, causing individuals to re-examine their relationship with the divine or with the world around them.

- Faith Renewal: For others, periods of spiritual dryness or disillusionment may give way to a renewal of faith, where new meaning and purpose are discovered through reflection, community, or spiritual practice.

1.4 Faith in Various Contexts: Manifestations Across Religions and Spiritual Practices

Faith is expressed differently depending on the religious or cultural context, but certain core elements remain consistent across traditions. Below is a comparison of how faith manifests in monotheistic, polytheistic, and secular contexts.

Comparative Analysis of Faith in Monotheistic vs. Polytheistic Religions

- Monotheistic Religions: Faith in monotheistic traditions like Christianity, Judaism, and Islam revolves around belief in a single, all-powerful deity. A personal relationship with God, strict moral codes, and an emphasis on obedience to divine will often characterize faith. Worship is typically focused on devotion to one supreme being, and faith includes the belief in revelation through sacred texts. By the way, in case you didn't know, these three religions have more in common than just being monotheistic. Christianity was a sect of Judaism. The pivotal figures in both faiths, Isaac(Christianity) and Ismael (Islam) were half-brothers by their father, Abraham(Jews). It is said that Ishmael and Abraham together rebuilt the Kaaba in Mecca, now Islam's holiest site. In a nutshell, Jews do not believe Jesus was the Messiah, and Islam believes he was a prophet like Mohammed, and the Messiah is still at large.

- Polytheistic Religions: In polytheistic traditions, such as Hinduism or ancient Greek and Roman religions, faith is more fluid, often involving multiple gods with different functions or attributes. Believers may have a personal devotion to one deity while acknowledging others. Faith in polytheism tends to be more pluralistic, emphasizing rituals, mythology, and practices rather than strict adherence to a singular doctrine. The Eastern approach to God is an inner journey toward the center of one's being. It is living in the present, fully aware of yourself and your surroundings. It's almost a permanent self-help cycle.

Faith in Secular Contexts: Spirituality Without Organized Religion

Faith is not confined to religious institutions. In secular contexts, many people still experience forms of faith, albeit outside traditional religious structures.

- Spiritual but Not Religious: Many individuals identify as "spiritual but not religious" (SBNR), finding faith in personal spiritual practices like meditation, mindfulness, or connection to nature. Faith here may be centered on concepts like universal love, energy, or cosmic interconnectedness without adherence to a specific dogma or deity.

- Humanistic Faith: Secular faith can also manifest as a belief in humanity, social justice, or ethical principles. For example, some people place their trust in the potential for human progress, compassion, or moral responsibility, viewing these as sources of meaning and purpose.

A Holistic Understanding of Faith

Faith, in its most total sense, is a complex, evolving journey that encompasses cognitive, emotional, and social elements. It is a dynamic process that grows and transforms with life's experiences, shaped by community, tradition, and personal reflection. Whether within the confines of a religion or outside of it, faith is a profound force that influences how individuals perceive the world, make decisions, and find meaning in their lives.

By understanding faith in its various dimensions and contexts, we gain insight into its enduring power to connect us to something larger—whether that be a divine being, a cosmic order, or the shared humanity that binds us together

Doubt as a Catalyst: Embracing Uncertainty

Doubt is often perceived as a threat to belief, a shadow cast across faith, a force that undermines faith and certainty. However, doubt can also be a positive and remodeling force, that leads to better understanding and personal growth. Philosophers like Descartes have long championed doubt as a fundamental tool in the search for truth. Descartes' method of doubt, which involves questioning everything until only certainty remains, illustrates the importance of doubt in refining our convictions. This philosophical approach encourages us to strip away assumptions and rebuild our beliefs on a solid foundation. Rather than viewing it solely as a negative experience, we can learn to embrace doubt as a necessary part of spiritual and intellectual development. By confronting and engaging with doubt, individuals can strengthen their beliefs, evolve their thinking, and cultivate resilience in the face of this discomfort While uncertainty.

1.5 Doubt as a Positive Force: A Pathway to Growth

Psychologically, doubt can be both unsettling and liberating. It introduces cognitive dissonance, the mental tension of holding contradictory beliefs. This discomfort, while initially distressing, can foster flexibility as we work to reconcile opposing ideas. Over time, we learn to navigate the emotional turmoil that doubt brings— fear, anxiety, and uncertainty—transforming it into a source of strength. By confronting our doubts head-on, we build a mental fortitude that strengthens our faith. Resilience is not about avoiding doubt but learning to live with it.

- Questioning Assumptions: Doubt encourages individuals to question long-held beliefs or ideas that may no longer serve them. By examining these beliefs critically, they can uncover inconsistencies or gaps in understanding, leading to a more mature and refined worldview.

- Promoting Humility: Embracing doubt fosters intellectual humility. It reminds us that certainty is elusive and that there is always more to learn. This humility opens the door to deeper inquiry, curiosity, and empathy for others who hold different views.

- Personal Growth Through Challenge: By facing doubt head-on, individuals are often propelled into a period of personal transformation. The process of grappling with uncertainty strengthens critical thinking, builds emotional resilience, and leads to a more nuanced and authentic relationship with one's beliefs.

- **Personal Growth Through Questioning: Stories of Individuals Who Grew from Doubt**

There are countless stories of individuals who have gone through periods of deep doubt only to emerge with a stronger, more refined sense of self or belief. For example, religious figures such as Mother Teresa, who expressed profound doubt in her letters, still found meaning and purpose through their struggles. Similarly, public figures like Martin Luther King Jr. navigated moments of doubt and despair but channeled them into resilience and renewed commitment to their causes. Doubt, in these cases, did not diminish their greatness; instead, it became a source of strength and clarity.

1.6 The Role of Doubt in Faith Development

In faith development, doubt is not an obstacle to overcome but a necessary part of the journey. Doubt prompts individuals to question simplistic or inherited beliefs, allowing for more profound spiritual growth.

Doubt in Religious Texts: Examples from Major World Religions

In the vast tapestry of religious thought, the Abrahamic religions—Christianity, Judaism, and Islam—have long grappled with the concept of doubt:

- **Christianity:** The Bible's "Doubting Thomas" story is a famous example. After Jesus' resurrection, Thomas expressed doubt and needed tangible proof to believe. Rather than condemning him, Jesus gently affirmed his need to question, offering him the evidence he sought. This story underscores the idea that doubt is a part of faith and can lead to enhanced conviction.

- **Buddhism**: In Buddhist teachings, doubt (vicikicchā) is acknowledged as one of the "Five Hindrances" to enlightenment, but it is also seen as an opportunity for deeper reflection. Rather than dismissing doubt, practitioners are encouraged to engage with it, questioning the teachings to arrive at their own understanding. It also embraces the concept of "not knowing," viewing doubt not as a barrier but as a path to enlightenment. The Zen koan is a paradoxical statement or question designed to provoke doubt and challenge conventional thinking, leading to moments of insight. This practice underscores the belief that certainty is an illusion and proper understanding comes from embracing the unknown.

- **Islam:** The Quran features verses that remind believers of the importance of contemplation and reflection. For instance, Surah 29:20 encourages believers to "travel through the earth and see how He began creation." This call to inquiry implies that doubt and curiosity are integral parts of understanding divine truth.

- **The Talmudic tradition:** rich with debate and discussion, encourages the faithful to question and seek deeper understanding, demonstrating that doubt can lead to greater wisdom.

- **Indigenous and earth-based traditions:** Doubt is often woven into oral narratives that reflect the complexities of human experience. Such narratives do not provide easy answers but invite reflection and dialogue, encouraging individuals to find meaning in the process of questioning.

Stages of Faith Development: How Doubt Propels Movement from One Stage to the Next

James Fowler, a psychologist known for his work on faith development, described various stages of faith from childhood through adulthood. Doubt plays a crucial role in moving from one stage to the next:

- Stage 0: Primal Faith (Infancy) Birth to 2 years. This is the pre-stage of faith development. Faith is often simplistic and rule-based in the early stages of life, tied to familial or cultural traditions. Children tend to adopt the beliefs and practices of their parents and communities, often viewing faith in black-and-white terms—right vs. wrong, good vs. evil.

- Stage 1: Intuitive-Projective Faith (Early Childhood) 2 to 7 years. During this stage, faith is shaped by imagination and intuition. Children are highly influenced by the stories, images, and behaviors of those around them, such as parents, caregivers, and religious figures. Concepts of God and spirituality are often anthropomorphized and shaped by fantasy and experiences, with little distinction between reality and imagination.

- **Stage 2: Mythic-Literal Faith (Middle Childhood)** 7 to 12 years. At this stage, children begin to take religious stories and symbols more literally. They start understanding the world through concrete thinking and grasp moral rules and religious narratives in a very literal sense. Religious symbols are seen as facts, and metaphors or abstract concepts may be misunderstood or overly simplified.

- Stage 3: Synthetic-Conventional Faith (Adolescence) Typically begins around 12 years. In this stage, faith is shaped by conformity to the values and beliefs of significant others (family, community, religion). External authorities influence adolescents and tend to develop a more coherent belief system but still lack critical analysis. Faith becomes more relational, with a desire to belong and be accepted. Individuals may have a deep emotional commitment to their beliefs but haven't examined them critically.

- Stage 4 (Individuative-Reflective Faith): Age: This stage often begins in the early 20s. It involves a personal reflection on one's beliefs and values, often triggered by life experiences. Individuals start questioning the authority of institutions, parents, and communities and begin to define their faith for themselves. They may become more self-aware, critically evaluating their inherited beliefs, and seek to understand the personal relevance of their faith.

- Stage 5 (Conjunctive Faith): Mid-30s and onward (may vary). People in this stage embrace paradox and mystery. They become more comfortable with ambiguity and accept that there may be truths beyond their own perspective. Faith is no longer about clear-cut answers but about a deeper understanding of complex, often conflicting truths. There's a greater openness to other beliefs, and individuals become more appreciative of diversity in spirituality and religion. Symbolic and metaphorical interpretations are more comfortable now.

- Stage 6: Universalizing Faith (Rare) Often associated with older adults, but few reach this stage. This stage is characterized by a selfless love for others and a deep sense of justice and compassion. Individuals in this stage transcend specific religious beliefs and live their faith in an all-encompassing way that focuses on universal principles like love, justice, and peace. People in this stage often become prophetic figures who challenge the status quo. Figures like Mahatma Gandhi, Martin Luther King Jr., or Mother Teresa are frequently cited as individuals who might have reached this level of faith development.

The Psychological Impacts of Doubt

While doubt can be life-altering, it often comes with psychological challenges. Doubt can cause discomfort and emotional turmoil, but individuals can develop resilience and strength by learning to manage these struggles.

Cognitive Dissonance: The Mental Struggle of Holding Conflicting Beliefs

Doubt often results in cognitive dissonance—a psychological state in which individuals hold conflicting beliefs or values. This dissonance can be deeply uncomfortable as the mind seeks to reconcile the inconsistency.

- Example: A person may have been raised in a religious tradition that teaches specific moral rules. However, as they grow older, they may encounter experiences or ideas that contradict those teachings. The tension between old beliefs and new insights can create mental strain, forcing the individual to either adjust their beliefs or experience ongoing discomfort.

Resilience Building: Overcoming Doubt to Strengthen Belief

Doubt, when managed constructively, can lead to greater resilience. Overcoming challenges to one's faith or beliefs fosters psychological strength modern secularization trend as individuals learn to accept ambiguity and uncertainty without being overwhelmed.

- Reconciliation of Doubt: People who have navigated doubt often emerge with a more flexible and resilient mindset. They learn that faith is not about certainty but about trust in the face of uncertainty. This resilience helps them face future challenges with greater composure and confidence.

Emotional Turmoil: Navigating Feelings of Fear and Anxiety

Doubt often brings with it intense emotions, including fear, anxiety, and even despair. These feelings can be disorienting but are also a normal part of the process.

- Fear of Being Wrong: Many people experience anxiety over the possibility that their doubts may lead them away from long-held beliefs. They fear losing their sense of identity or the support of their community.

- Embracing the Unknown: Learning to sit with this emotional turmoil without seeking immediate answers can be a powerful exercise in emotional growth. Over time, individuals often find that their doubts lead them to greater inner peace and acceptance of life's uncertainties.

1.7 Cultural and Historical Influences on Belief Systems

Faith doesn't exist in a vacuum. It ebbs and flows with culture, reflecting the values and priorities of the societies that hold it. In different cultural contexts, faith takes on unique flavors. For instance, the communal nature of African spirituality emphasizes a collective experience of the divine, contrasting with the individualism often found in Western Christianity. These cultural influences shape how religious practices are expressed and adapted over time. Consider how Buddhism, originally rooted in the Indian subcontinent, transformed as it spread across Asia. In Japan, it merged with Shinto to create a distinctive blend that reflects local customs and beliefs. This cultural adaptation ensures that faith remains relevant and vibrant, allowing it to speak to the hearts of its followers in a language they understand.

Historical events also play a significant role in reshaping belief systems. The Reformation, a seismic shift in Christian history, challenged the authority of the Catholic Church and gave rise to Protestantism. This movement altered religious doctrine and democratized faith, emphasizing personal interpretation of scripture. Such historical shifts demonstrate how belief systems adapt to new realities, often catalyzed by social and political change. Similarly, the modern secularization trend reflects how faith practices must navigate the complexities of an increasingly scientific and rational world. As societies move towards secular values, religious practices evolve, often becoming more personal and less institutional in nature.

Culture can be a double-edged sword when it comes to doubt. Some cultures view doubt as a taboo, a threat to the stability of communal beliefs. In these contexts, questioning can be seen as a betrayal, stifling exploration and growth. Yet, history shows us that movements encouraging skepticism, such as the Enlightenment, have paved the way for progress. The Enlightenment championed reason and empirical evidence, challenging traditional religious authority and promoting a culture of questioning. This period of intellectual awakening emphasized the importance of doubt in the pursuit of knowledge, setting the stage for modern skepticism. It is this interplay between culture and doubt that often determines whether questioning is suppressed or celebrated.

1.8 Strategies for Embracing Doubt

To navigate doubt constructively, individuals can use practical strategies to reflect, process, and engage with their uncertainties.

Journaling and Reflection: Tools for Processing Doubt

One of the most effective ways to work through doubt is by journaling. Writing down thoughts, questions, and reflections allows individuals to clarify their thinking and gain perspective.

- Self-Reflection: Regular journaling helps people track the evolution of their doubts, noting how their perspectives shift over time. This process can provide reassurance that doubt is not a permanent state but part of a more extensive journey.

- Spiritual Journaling: Some individuals find documenting prayers, meditations, or spiritual insights as helpful when they wrestle with doubt. This practice can deepen their spiritual awareness and provide a tangible record of their growth.

- Open dialogue with trusted individuals or communities is another fundamental strategy for navigating doubt. Sharing doubts with others helps normalize the experience and offers alternative perspectives.

- Safe Spaces: Finding a community or support group that encourages open conversations about doubt can be incredibly healing. Engaging in these discussions with others who have experienced similar struggles creates a sense of belonging and reduces the isolation often associated with doubt.

- Mentors or Spiritual Guides: Seeking guidance from a mentor or spiritual leader who is comfortable with ambiguity can provide reassurance and wisdom during times of uncertainty.

5. Embracing Doubt as a Path to Growth

Doubt is not the enemy of belief but a catalyst for deeper understanding, personal growth, and resilience. By embracing doubt and engaging with it constructively, individuals can break free from simplistic thinking and experience a more authentic, mature relationship with their beliefs. Whether through philosophical inquiry, personal stories, or faith development, doubt ultimately leads to a deeper, more nuanced perspective on life's big questions.

Far from being a weakness, doubt is a sign of intellectual humility and spiritual openness. By viewing doubt as a natural and necessary part of growth, we empower ourselves to face uncertainty with courage, confidence, and resilience

1.9 Cultural Influences on Faith: Shaping Beliefs Across Contexts

Belief systems—whether religious, spiritual, or philosophical—are deeply embedded in the cultural and historical contexts from which they arise. As societies evolve, so too do the faith systems within them. Cultural norms, historical events, and societal shifts all play crucial roles in shaping, reinforcing, and sometimes challenging these beliefs. In this exploration, we will examine how cultural and historical influences mold belief systems, how they adapt over time, and how doubt interacts with these forces. Cultural context significantly shapes and reshapes faith, often determining how religious beliefs are interpreted, practiced, and transmitted. Faith traditions do not exist in isolation but are influenced by the values, norms, and practices of the societies in which they are situated.

Faith in Different Cultural Contexts: A Comparative Analysis

Religious beliefs and practices often vary widely depending on the cultural context in which they are expressed. This variance highlights the flexible nature of faith systems and their capacity to adapt to the cultural milieu.

- Christianity in the West vs. Africa: While Christianity in Western cultures often emphasizes individualism and personal salvation, in many African contexts, the faith takes on more communal forms, focusing on collective well-being and harmony within the community. The idea of healing, for instance, is often more central to African Christian practices, blending traditional healing methods with Christian teachings.

- Buddhism in Southeast Asia vs. the West: In Southeast Asia, Buddhism is deeply intertwined with cultural traditions and often includes rituals, offerings, and merit-making practices. In contrast, Western interpretations of Buddhism are frequently more focused on mindfulness, meditation, and individual spiritual development, often stripped of ritualistic elements.

Cultural Adaptation of Religious Practices: Examples from History

Throughout history, religious practices have adapted to fit new cultural realities, leading to the evolution of belief systems over time.

- Syncretism in Latin America: When Christianity was introduced to indigenous populations in Latin America during the colonial period, it often blended with local beliefs and practices. For instance, the figure of the Virgin of Guadalupe in Mexico became a powerful symbol that combined elements of indigenous spirituality with Catholic devotion. This syncretism allowed indigenous cultures to maintain aspects of their spiritual heritage while adopting new religious beliefs.

- Islam and Local Customs: As Islam spread across various regions, it adapted to local cultural practices. In parts of Indonesia and Malaysia, Islamic practices have integrated aspects of indigenous customs, creating a distinct blend of faith expressions that reflect both Islamic doctrine and local traditions, such as the use of traditional arts in religious ceremonies.

1.10 Historical Shifts in Belief Systems: How Events Shape Faith Narratives

Historical events often act as turning points in the evolution of belief systems. Wars, revolutions, philosophical movements, and technological advancements all leave their mark on how faith is understood and practiced.

The Reformation: Its Impact on Christian Beliefs

The Protestant Reformation in the 16th century is a prime example of how historical events can radically transform belief systems. Sparked by Martin Luther's 95 Theses, the Reformation led to a dramatic shift in Christian thought and practice, challenging the authority of the Catholic Church and introducing new theological ideas.

- Shift in Doctrine: The Reformation brought about new interpretations of core Christian beliefs, particularly concerning salvation, scripture, and the role of the clergy. The concept of sola fide (faith alone) emerged, emphasizing that faith, rather than works, was the path to salvation. This marked a significant departure from Catholic teachings at the time.

- Impact on Religious Practice: The Reformation also democratized religious practice, encouraging individuals to read and interpret the Bible for themselves rather than relying on the clergy. This shift profoundly altered the relationship between the believer and the church, laying the foundation for the development of various Protestant denominations.

Secularization Trends: How Modernity Influences Religious Practice

Modernity, with its emphasis on reason, scientific progress, and individual autonomy, has contributed to the secularization of many societies, leading to a decline in traditional religious observance in certain regions, particularly in the West.

- Enlightenment Influence: The Enlightenment's focus on reason and empirical evidence challenged traditional religious authority. Thinkers like Voltaire and Kant questioned the role of organized religion in society, advocating for a separation of church and state and promoting religious tolerance. This intellectual movement laid the groundwork for secularism in modern Europe and North America.

- Modern Secularization: In contemporary societies, secularization trends continue to influence religious practice. In many European countries, church attendance has declined significantly, and religious institutions no longer wield the same political or cultural power they once did. In contrast, other regions, like parts of the Global South, continue to experience religious growth and fervor, highlighting the complex relationship between modernity and faith.

1.11 The Interplay Between Culture and Doubt: Suppression and Encouragement

Cultural norms can shape not only belief systems but also how doubt is perceived and addressed. In some societies, doubt is suppressed and seen as taboo, while in others, questioning and skepticism are encouraged as part of intellectual and spiritual growth.

Cultural Taboos: Doubt as a Forbidden Topic

In many traditional or conservative societies, doubt is often viewed as a threat to social cohesion and moral order. Questioning religious or cultural norms can lead to ostracism, punishment, or suppression.

- Islamic Contexts: In some conservative Islamic cultures, open expressions of doubt or apostasy are heavily discouraged, and questioning religious authorities can result in social isolation or legal consequences. This has created environments where individuals struggle to express their doubts openly for fear of societal repercussions.

- Christian Fundamentalism: In certain evangelical or fundamentalist Christian communities, questioning core doctrines (such as the Bible's inerrancy) is often seen as a sign of spiritual weakness or rebellion. This can create an atmosphere where doubt is stifled, leading individuals to internalize their uncertainties rather than engage with them constructively.

Movements Encouraging Questioning: The Enlightenment and Modern Skepticism

While some cultures suppress doubt, others have embraced it as a necessary part of intellectual and spiritual development. The Enlightenment, for example, encouraged skepticism, inquiry, and questioning of traditional authorities.

- Enlightenment Philosophy: Thinkers such as David Hume and Immanuel Kant promoted the idea that doubt and skepticism were essential tools for discovering truth. Their writings encouraged people to question religious doctrines and seek answers through reason and evidence. This intellectual shift profoundly influenced Western thought, leading to an era of scientific inquiry and philosophical debate that valued doubt as a virtue.

- Modern Skepticism: In contemporary times, movements like the New Atheism (promoted by figures such as Richard Dawkins and Sam Harris) have further encouraged skepticism, particularly in relation to religious belief. These movements argue that doubt is not only acceptable but necessary for intellectual and moral progress.

1.12 The Impact of Globalization: Interconnectedness and the Evolution of Belief Systems

Globalization has brought unprecedented levels of association between people, cultures, and belief systems. This exchange of ideas has influenced how individuals and communities approach faith, leading to both increased religious pluralism and opportunities for interfaith dialogue.

Interfaith Dialogue: Encouraging Understanding Across Cultures

As different religious and spiritual traditions come into closer contact through globalization, interfaith dialogue has become a key tool for fostering mutual understanding and respect between different communities.

- Building Bridges: Interfaith organizations and initiatives encourage people from different religious backgrounds to engage in open, respectful dialogue. This process helps to break down stereotypes, dispel misconceptions, and promote cooperation between diverse faith groups.

- Examples: Events like the Parliament of the World's Religions or organizations such as the United Religions Initiative promote interfaith dialogue, bringing together religious leaders and laypeople from around the world to discuss shared values and common challenges.

Global Exchange of Ideas: The Internet as a Facilitator of Faith Discussion

The advent of the internet has transformed the way individuals engage with belief systems, offering new platforms for both questioning and affirming faith.

- Online Communities: Through social media, forums, and websites, people can now explore a variety of belief systems, share their doubts, and seek answers from others across the globe. This has led to a more globalized and diverse religious experience, where individuals can access spiritual teachings from other traditions and engage in conversations that were once limited by geography.

- Increased Access to Information: The internet has democratized access to religious and philosophical texts, allowing individuals to engage with a broad range of ideas, from ancient scriptures to modern theological debates. This ease of access has contributed to the spread of secularism in some areas while also fueling the growth of new religious movements in others.

1.13 The Dynamic Relationship Between Culture, History, and Faith

Cultural and historical contexts play a profound role in shaping belief systems. From the adaptation of religious practices to historical events like the Reformation and the Enlightenment, belief systems continuously evolve in response to the changing world around them. At the same time, doubt—both suppressed and encouraged—interacts with these cultural forces, pushing individuals to question, grow, and redefine their faith.

In an increasingly interconnected world, globalization is reshaping belief systems by fostering interfaith dialogue and creating new avenues for the exploration of faith and doubt. As cultures continue to engage with one another, the global exchange of ideas will undoubtedly further transform how individuals and communities experience belief. Through this dynamic interplay, faith continues to be a living, evolving force shaped by both cultural tradition and modern innovation.

CHAPTER 2

THE EMOTIONAL LANDSCAPE OF FAITH TRANSITIONS

Transitioning through faith, whether it's questioning long-held beliefs or moving toward a new spiritual path, can feel like an emotional rollercoaster. The highs and lows experienced during this time are often intense and profound, affecting every aspect of one's emotional and psychological well-being. Faith, for many, provides a sense of identity, community, and purpose, so shifting away from or reevaluating those beliefs can create a whirlwind of emotions ranging from excitement to fear and even deep confusion.

2.1 The Emotional Highs and Lows: Intense Reactions to Questioning Faith

A faith transition often begins with a mixture of exhilaration and anxiety as new perspectives are explored and familiar belief systems are questioned. This duality creates a wave of emotional extremes that can be difficult to navigate.

Initial Excitement: The Thrill of Discovering New Perspectives

The beginning of a faith transition may bring a sense of wonder and excitement. Discovering new ideas or spiritual paths can feel liberating, especially when they resonate on a deeply personal level. Many experience a burst of intellectual and emotional energy as they explore these new perspectives. On the other hand, a transition forced by disappointment, lack of understanding, or a traumatic event can be paralyzing.

- Feeling Inspired: New beliefs or frameworks may inspire intellectual excitement as they challenge old assumptions and offer fresh ways to see the world. The possibility of finding a more authentic spiritual path or even leaving behind dogmatic teachings can create a sense of personal empowerment.

- Opening Up: When people connect with others who share similar questions or new beliefs, they often feel they belong to a broader, more inclusive community. This connection can bring relief and validation, as they know they're not alone in their journey.

Fear of the Unknown: Anxiety About Leaving Behind Familiar Beliefs

However, the excitement of discovery is often tempered by fear. Leaving behind familiar beliefs can create anxiety about the future, especially when those beliefs have provided comfort, security, or a clear sense of direction in life.

- Fear of Losing Identity: Faith is deeply tied to one's sense of identity; questioning it can feel like a loss of self. People often worry about who they will become if they abandon their current beliefs.

- Fear of Social Repercussions: Changing faith or leaving behind religious communities can bring fears of judgment, rejection, or alienation from family, friends, and religious communities. The possibility of isolation adds another layer of anxiety to the transition process.

2.2 Common Emotional Experiences in Faith Transition

The emotional landscape of a faith transition is complex and many-sided. It often involves a combination of confusion, fear, relief, and guilt, making it a highly charged and personal experience.

Confusion and Doubt: Feeling Lost Without a Clear Belief System

One of the most common emotions during a faith transition is confusion. Without the clarity of a familiar belief system, people going through this experience may feel unmoored and directionless, both emotionally and intellectually.

- Existential Confusion: Many people ask themselves fundamental questions like "What is the meaning of life?" or "How do I know what's true?" These existential concerns can provoke deep confusion as the old frameworks that provided answers are no longer viable.

- Doubt and Ambiguity: Constantly questioning beliefs can lead to a state of uncertainty, which is deeply uncomfortable for many. The sense of not knowing or doubting everything they once held dear can provoke feelings of instability.

My journey away from religion began after my dad passed away. We had recently converted from Catholicism to Baptist, and my dad enthusiastically embraced this new faith. He transformed into a different person, giving up excessive drinking, smoking, womanizing, and partying. He spent more quality time with us, and even though we didn't have much, he was genuinely happy. He even donated his musical instruments to the church. Then he died.

As a young child, I couldn't understand why this happened, nor could my mom. Our lives were forever changed. Mom felt lost, dragging me along in her search for answers to questions I couldn't even articulate. No one asked me what I felt, but my biggest question was: why now? Just as he had finally gotten his life together, he was taken away. I felt angry with both my dad and God. Why would he leave us? Why would God take him, especially knowing what we would face after his death?

As the years went by, those questions lingered. New ones emerged as we explored various faiths: Rosicrucians, Gnostics, back to Catholicism, Voodoo, evangelicals, and countless obscure sects that I struggle to remember. Seeking answers from leaders of these groups only deepened my confusion, as we were often met with judgment for our doubts. My main complaint is precisely here. The leaders who were supposed to make us feel better were making things worse, and then, one day, I quit going to church and looking for answers and concentrated on surviving each day, hoping the next would be better.

My mom is now 80 years old and deeply believes in God outside any religion. As for me, I grew up, lived my life, developed many unhealthy coping mechanisms, and I'm still looking.

Relief and Liberation: The Freedom Found in Questioning Established Doctrines

On the other hand, faith transitions can also bring an enormous sense of relief. Questioning rigid doctrines or beliefs can feel like breaking free for those who feel restricted, burdened, or judged by them.

- Letting Go of Guilt or Shame: For some, questioning their faith allows them to let go of teachings that made them feel guilty or inadequate, particularly around moral or lifestyle choices that were once condemned by their previous religious communities.

- Discovering Authenticity: Many find liberation in embracing their doubts and uncertainties, allowing them to pursue a spiritual path that feels more aligned with their true selves. This process often brings a sense of empowerment and inner peace.

Fear of Divine Retribution: Worries About Spiritual Consequences

For those raised in religious traditions that emphasize divine punishment or eternal consequences, the fear of spiritual retribution can be overwhelming.

- Fear of Hell or Punishment: Individuals from conservative or fundamentalist backgrounds may worry that by questioning or leaving their faith, they are risking eternal punishment. This fear can cause intense emotional conflict, particularly when the desire for truth conflicts with fear-based teachings.

- Struggling with Guilt: Even when intellectually moving away from a faith tradition, emotional ties to teachings about guilt and retribution can linger, creating emotional dissonance and inner turmoil.

2.3 The Psychological Impact: How Emotional Turmoil Affects Mental Health

The emotional highs and lows of a faith transition can take a severe toll on mental health, especially when the process feels overwhelming or when there is little support from others. The uncertainty and emotional upheaval can lead to stress, anxiety, and, in some cases, depression.

Stress and Anxiety: The Mental Toll of Spiritual Upheaval

The uncertainty that comes with questioning deeply held beliefs often leads to increased levels of stress and anxiety.

- Cognitive Dissonance: Individuals may experience cognitive dissonance—the mental discomfort arising from simultaneously holding conflicting beliefs or values. This can create a heightened sense of stress as people wrestle with the gap between their former beliefs and emerging perspectives.

- Fear of Rejection: Social anxiety can also increase as people worry about how their changing beliefs will affect their relationships with family, friends, and their broader religious community. This fear of rejection can amplify feelings of stress and isolation.

Depression and Hopelessness: When Transitions Feel Overwhelming

For some, the weight of a faith transition can lead to feelings of hopelessness, particularly if the process feels like a betrayal of their past selves or a loss of meaning.

- Loss of Purpose: Many people find that faith provides a clear sense of purpose or meaning in life, and without it, they may feel adrift or purposeless. This loss of direction can lead to feelings of hopelessness or depression.

- Spiritual Numbness: Some may feel emotionally detached or spiritually numb as they struggle to reconcile their changing beliefs with their previous identity. This emotional detachment can deepen feelings of depression, especially when the individual feels disconnected from a higher purpose or community.

2.4 Coping Strategies: Practical Advice for Managing Emotional Turmoil

Managing the emotional turmoil of a faith transition is challenging, but there are coping strategies that can help individuals navigate the process with greater emotional resilience and mental clarity.

Mindfulness Exercises: Techniques for Staying Grounded Amid Chaos

Mindfulness practices can be a powerful tool for managing emotional turbulence during a faith transition. By focusing on the present moment and observing thoughts and feelings without judgment, mindfulness can help individuals stay grounded.

- Breathing Exercises: Simple breathing exercises can help reduce anxiety and promote a sense of calm during moments of emotional upheaval. By slowing down the breath, individuals can activate their body's relaxation response, reducing stress and helping to clear the mind.

- Meditation: Meditation practices, especially those rooted in mindfulness or contemplation, can help individuals observe their doubts and fears from a place of non-attachment, fostering emotional resilience and mental clarity.

Professional Support: The Benefits of Counseling or Therapy

Faith transitions can bring up a range of deep emotional issues that may benefit from professional support. Therapists and counselors, mainly those trained in religious trauma or existential counseling, can provide a safe space to explore these complex emotions.

- Therapy for Religious Trauma: For individuals coming from fundamentalist or high-control religious environments, therapy can help address religious trauma, which often includes fear of divine punishment, guilt, and emotional abuse associated with religious teachings.

- Existential Counseling: This type of counseling focuses on helping individuals navigate life's big questions—purpose, meaning, and identity. It can be beneficial to those grappling with the loss of faith or the search for new spiritual meaning.

Faith transitions, though often fraught with emotional turmoil, can also be deeply transformative experiences. From the initial excitement of exploring new ideas to the confusion and fear of leaving behind familiar beliefs, this journey is rich with emotional complexity. By recognizing and accepting these emotional highs and lows, individuals can navigate the rollercoaster of faith transitions more constructively.

Coping strategies like mindfulness and professional support can help manage the mental toll of these transitions, offering tools to deal with the stress, anxiety, and depression that may arise. Ultimately, faith transitions offer the opportunity for personal growth, resilience, and the discovery of a more authentic spiritual path, even amidst the emotional chaos.

2.5 Personal Narratives of Faith and Doubt

The journey from devout belief to skepticism can be an emotionally and intellectually challenging process. Personal narratives of this transition reveal stories of transformation, where once faithful individuals begin questioning their long-held beliefs. These stories reflect the complexities of faith, doubt, and the search for meaning, offering insights into the struggles and ultimate resolutions of individuals facing a spiritual crossroads.

1. A Tale of Two Beliefs: From Faithful to Skeptic

Faith often forms the core of one's identity and worldview, making the transition from belief to skepticism is a profound and personal experience. This section delves into the stories of individuals who once held deep religious convictions but found themselves questioning the foundations of their faith.

Example: A Devout Christian Questioning Biblical Literalism

One story might follow a devout Christian who grew up in a conservative religious community emphasizing biblical literalism. Throughout their life, they embraced the Bible as the infallible word of God. However, as they pursued higher education, they encountered scientific evidence that conflicted with the creation story and other biblical narratives. This led to deep questioning of the Bible's literal accuracy and the role of metaphor or symbolism in sacred texts.

- Turning Point: The individual might recall a specific moment in college when they took a course on evolutionary biology, which directly challenged their understanding of Genesis. Faced with compelling evidence, they began to wrestle with whether the Bible could still hold spiritual truth if it weren't factually accurate in every aspect.

- Emotional Struggle: This led to a period of intense cognitive dissonance. They found themselves torn between loyalty to their faith community and the desire for intellectual honesty. Their faith, which had once been a source of comfort and certainty, became a source of anxiety and doubt.

Example: A Muslim Exploring Secular Humanism After a Personal Crisis

Another narrative might follow a Muslim who, after a series of personal tragedies, began to doubt the existence of an all-powerful, benevolent deity. The death of a close family member in an unexpected accident prompted them to question how an all-merciful God could allow such suffering.

- Turning Point: After a period of deep prayer and fasting for answers that never came, the individual began to explore secular philosophies, such as humanism, that offered a non-religious framework for making sense of suffering and ethics.

- Emotional Struggle: Their transition was marked by a profound sense of loss, not just of faith, but of the community and identity that their religion had provided. They felt guilt for abandoning their belief system and a lingering fear of divine retribution, even as they found new ways of understanding the world.

2. Highlighting Key Turning Points: Shifting from Belief to Skepticism

In each narrative, pivotal moments trigger a shift from deep faith to doubt. These turning points, often intellectual, emotional, or experiential, spark the internal process of questioning once-solid beliefs.

Encountering Scientific Evidence that Challenges Religious Teachings

For many, exposure to new ideas or scientific evidence that contradicts religious teachings can be the catalyst for doubt. For the Christian who questioned biblical literalism, learning about the scientific method, evolution, and cosmology played a significant role in reshaping their worldview.

- Conflict with Creationism: The realization that the Earth is billions of years old, in contrast to the 6,000-year timeline supported by their faith community, forced a reevaluation of what was seen as divine truth versus human interpretation.

- The Struggle for Reconciliation: Initially, the individual may have tried to reconcile their faith with scientific knowledge, exploring the possibility that both could coexist. However, as questions multiplied, it became clear that their religious framework could no longer account for the empirical evidence they encountered.

Personal Experiences of Perceived Religious Hypocrisy

For others, it's not intellectual discovery but personal experience that sows the seeds of doubt. The Muslim narrative might describe how an individual's personal crisis—perhaps involving a religious leader's moral failure or the perceived indifference of their faith community during a time of need—began to crack the foundation of their faith.

- The Role of Community Failings: When religious institutions fail to live up to their moral ideals, it can be deeply disillusioning for believers. Witnessing or experiencing hypocrisy among religious leaders or communities may cause individuals to question the integrity of the teachings they've been following.

3. The Emotional and Intellectual Struggles of Transition

As faith is questioned, the internal conflict between belief and doubt can be emotionally wrenching. The intellectual tension between new evidence and old beliefs often mirrors an emotional struggle between fear, guilt, and the search for new meaning.

Cognitive Dissonance: Reconciling New Ideas with Old Beliefs

Cognitive dissonance occurs when individuals hold two contradictory beliefs, values, or ideas. For those transitioning from faith to skepticism, this tension often arises when new evidence or experiences directly conflict with long-held religious doctrines.

- Intellectual Discomfort: The Christian individual in our narrative may experience intellectual discomfort as they try to reconcile their belief in biblical literalism with scientific discoveries. The ongoing internal battle between religious faith and rational inquiry creates mental stress, leading them to question not only specific doctrines but the entire framework of their belief system.

Emotional Turmoil: Coping with Loss of Spiritual Identity

Emotionally, the transition from faith to skepticism can be as devastating as the intellectual conflict. For many, faith is not just about belief in God but about belonging to a community, finding purpose, and identifying with a larger story. Losing that faith can feel like a loss of self.

- Fear and Guilt: The Muslim individual might struggle with the emotional consequences of leaving behind their religious identity. Despite finding comfort in secular humanism, they may still feel residual fear of divine punishment or guilt for turning away from their faith.

- Loss of Community: Religious communities often provide a strong support system. Leaving behind that network, whether by choice or rejection, can lead to isolation and loneliness. Individuals may grieve not just their lost faith but the community and identity that came with it.

2.6 Resolutions and Outcomes: Finding a New Sense of Understanding

While the journey from faith to skepticism is often marked by struggle, it can also lead to new understandings and ways of living. Individuals find peace, community, and meaning in various ways, whether embracing uncertainty or finding new belief systems that resonate with their experiences.

Embracing Agnosticism as a Path of Inquiry

For some, like the Christian individual, the resolution may come as agnosticism. Rather than seeking absolute answers, they might find comfort in embracing uncertainty, seeing doubt not as a failure of faith but as an ongoing journey of exploration.

- Living with Uncertainty: Instead of rigidly adhering to doctrines, this individual may adopt an agnostic approach, remaining open to various possibilities while focusing on the questions rather than definitive answers. This shift often leads to a more flexible, less dogmatic way of engaging with spirituality and the world.

For the Muslim individual, the resolution might come through secular humanism, where they find both intellectual and emotional fulfillment. Joining secular organizations, whether focused on ethics, humanitarian efforts, or social justice, can provide a sense of community and purpose outside traditional religious structures.

- Secular Support Networks: Those in transition may discover a new sense of belonging and purpose by joining groups that focus on shared human values rather than specific religious beliefs. These communities often emphasize ethics, compassion, and personal responsibility without theological baggage, providing a supportive space.

2.7 Rediscovering Belief After Crisis

Imagine the scene: a quiet hospital room, sterile and still, where time seems to stretch endlessly. It was here that he sat, grappling with the unexpected loss of a loved one, an event that shattered the very foundations of his faith. The questions came like waves, relentless and unyielding. Where was the divine in this moment of despair? How could beliefs that had once felt so steadfast now seem so fragile? This was a crisis of faith, a profound unraveling that left him questioning everything he thought I knew. The emotional turmoil was palpable, a heavy mix of anger, confusion, and grief that seemed to have no end. Yet, amid this desolation, there lay the possibility of rediscovery, a chance to rebuild and redefine what faith truly meant.

Reconstructing belief after such a crisis is not a straightforward path. My own struggle after my dad died led my mother and I to seek out different faiths and denominations, as I mentioned earlier. Each new exploration was like a piece of a puzzle, gradually coming together to form a more complete picture. But the disappointment persisted. The mix of faiths and the dissimilar doctrines was confusing for my young mind. So it was that I wandered further and further away from any faith. The way back has been a tumultuous journey.

The Deconstruction Process: Unraveling and Rebuilding Beliefs

The deconstruction of faith is a deeply personal process marked by a systematic dismantling of long-held beliefs. It begins quietly, often unnoticed at first—a subtle questioning of the doctrines that once seemed inviolable. This journey often begins with questioning the very foundations of one's faith, progresses through a thorough reevaluation of doctrines and morals, and culminates in a reconstruction phase where new beliefs are formed. Along the way, individuals encounter challenges and revelations that shape their evolving spiritual identity.

As the old structures of belief crumble, the daunting task of rebuilding emerges.

1. Illustrating the Deconstruction Journey

Deconstruction refers to the process of critically examining and systematically dismantling the beliefs, doctrines, and practices one has been raised with or previously accepted. It's an intellectual, emotional, and sometimes spiritual process that allows individuals to confront contradictions or inadequacies within their belief systems.

Questioning Foundational Doctrines

One of the first steps in the deconstruction process often involves revisiting the core teachings of a religion with a critical lens. This can include religious texts, institutional teachings, or doctrinal tenets that were once accepted without question.

- Examining Religious Texts Critically: Individuals may question the literal truth of sacred texts, wondering whether specific stories are illustrative rather than factual or whether the moral teachings they contain are applicable in modern society. For example, a Christian might start to explore historical inconsistencies in the Bible or question the portrayal of gender roles in scripture.

- Reevaluating Moral Teachings: As part of the deconstruction process, individuals may also reassess the moral values imparted by their religious upbringing. They might examine whether those values align with their current understanding of ethics and human rights. For instance, someone raised in a tradition with rigid views on sexuality might seek to reconcile their faith's teachings with a more inclusive and equitable approach to relationships.

Example:

A person raised in a conservative faith community that espouses traditional gender roles might begin to question whether these roles are truly divinely ordained or simply a product of historical context. As they reevaluate these teachings, they may experience a shift in how they view gender, equality, and the broader moral framework of their faith.

2. Examining Catalysts for Deconstruction

The deconstruction process is often triggered by key life experiences or external influences that prompt individuals to rethink their beliefs. These catalysts vary widely but can include academic experiences, diverse cultural interactions, or personal crises.

Academic Exposure

For many, exposure to higher education or new ideas serves as the initial spark for deconstruction. University settings, in particular, often introduce individuals to critical thinking, alternative viewpoints, and scientific frameworks that challenge their pre-existing beliefs.

- The Role of Education: When individuals are exposed to academic disciplines like history, philosophy, and science, they may start to see inconsistencies in their faith or religious narratives. Higher education promotes inquiry, skepticism, and intellectual rigor, which can directly clash with faith traditions that emphasize unquestioning belief.

Diverse Interactions

Cultural and interfaith exposure can also be a powerful catalyst for deconstruction. Interacting with individuals from different religious or secular backgrounds may call one's own beliefs into question.

- Exposure to Different Cultures: Traveling, working, or forming relationships with people from diverse backgrounds can broaden perspectives. For example, a person raised in a monotheistic religion may encounter polytheistic or atheist worldviews that challenge the exclusivity or supremacy of their belief system.

Example:

A Muslim woman who moves to a more secular country for work might experience a shift in her worldview after being immersed in a society that values individual freedom over strict adherence to religious practices. Her encounters with different belief systems and lifestyles might prompt her to question the moral and cultural teachings she grew up with.

3. The Rebuilding Phase: Reconstructing Beliefs Post-Deconstruction

The second part of the deconstruction process involves rebuilding—developing a new set of beliefs, ethics, or philosophies after dismantling the old system. This stage is deeply personal and unique, with individuals drawing from various sources to create a worldview that resonates with them.

Formulating Personal Spirituality

After deconstruction, individuals often begin to explore spirituality in a more individualized and personalized way. This can involve rejecting organized religion altogether or adopting a more flexible and eclectic approach to faith.

- Developing a Unique Belief System: Some people choose to integrate aspects of their former faith into a more nuanced, personal spirituality. Others may explore entirely new spiritual practices, such as mindfulness, meditation, or New Age philosophies. The focus often shifts from external dogma to internal, experiential forms of spirituality.

Integrating New Philosophies

In the rebuilding phase, individuals might draw upon a wide range of philosophies and belief systems—religious or secular—to create a new framework for understanding the world.

- Adopting New Schools of Thought: Philosophies like secular humanism, existentialism, or even Buddhist teachings might be adopted to fill the intellectual and emotional gaps left by deconstruction. Individuals may also find value in adopting a non-religious ethical system that emphasizes human flourishing, empathy, and reason.

Example:

A former evangelical Christian might reconstruct their beliefs around a more agnostic or deistic perspective, focusing less on specific religious dogma and more on universal moral principles like kindness and justice. They may find meaning in exploring multiple spiritual traditions, incorporating elements from Eastern philosophies or nature-based practices.

4. Challenges and Revelations During the Deconstruction and Reconstruction Phases

The process of deconstructing and rebuilding one's faith is often filled with emotional and social challenges, but it can also lead to profound personal revelations and growth.

Isolation from Religious Communities

One of the primary challenges individuals face during deconstruction is a sense of isolation. Leaving behind a religious community can create feelings of loneliness, as these communities often provide a sense of belonging, identity, and support.

- Navigating Loneliness: As individuals question or leave their faith, they may feel cut off from family members, friends, or religious institutions that no longer share their views. The loss of community can be one of the most painful aspects of the deconstruction process, as it often involves severing ties with people or institutions that once played an important role in their lives.

Revelations of Self-Discovery

Despite the challenges, deconstruction often leads to important revelations about personal identity, purpose, and meaning. Through the process of questioning and rebuilding, individuals may discover a deeper sense of self and a new outlook on life.

- **Finding Meaning Beyond Organized Religion:** Many find that by stripping away dogma, they can reconnect with the core values and ethical principles that matter most to them. They may develop a sense of personal authenticity and empowerment, recognizing that their worth or purpose is not dependent on adherence to any particular religious institution.

The Deconstruction Process as a Path to Rebirth

The deconstruction and rebuilding of faith is a life-changing journey, one that involves intellectual questioning, emotional upheaval, and personal discovery. As individuals unravel their belief systems, they often encounter profound challenges, from isolation to cognitive dissonance. However, the process also offers immense opportunities for growth, self-understanding, and creating a more authentic, personally meaningful spiritual framework.

Whether individuals ultimately abandon organized religion or reshape their beliefs in new ways, the deconstruction process is an ongoing exploration of identity, values, and truth. It allows for a deeper understanding of the self and the world, as well as the freedom to construct a belief system that reflects one's unique journey and evolving sense of purpose.

CHAPTER 3

LEAVING RELIGION: STORIES OF SPIRITUAL INDEPENDENCE

The decision to leave organized religion is a profound and personal journey that reflects a deep search for spiritual independence. This chapter will explore the experiences of individuals who have consciously stepped away from their religious upbringings or long-held faith traditions, opting instead for a path defined by personal exploration, freedom from dogma, and a quest for authenticity. Through their stories, we will examine the reasons that lead people to leave organized religion, the challenges they face in doing so, and the benefits that come from embracing spiritual independence.

1. Narrating Experiences of Leaving Organized Religion

Many who leave organized religion do so not because they have lost faith in spirituality altogether, but because they seek a different, more authentic form of spiritual expression. These individuals often transition from structured, institutionalized faith traditions to alternative, more personal spiritual practices that align better with their evolving beliefs and values.

A Former Catholic Finding Solace in Nature-Based Spirituality

Take, for example, the story of a woman who grew up deeply rooted in the Catholic Church, finding solace in its rituals and community. Over time, however, she became increasingly disillusioned with the Church's hierarchical structure and teachings that felt rigid or disconnected from her personal experience of the divine. As she began exploring alternative spiritual paths, she found a deep connection to nature and Earth-based spirituality. Through practices like meditation in nature, seasonal celebrations, and connecting with the elements, she felt a newfound sense of peace and fulfillment outside the confines of organized religion.

An Ex-Jew Turning to Meditation as a Spiritual Practice

Similarly, consider the journey of a man raised in a conservative Jewish household, where religious traditions and community were central to his identity. After experiencing a personal crisis and feeling that his faith's teachings didn't offer the support or answers he needed, he began exploring mindfulness and meditation. In these practices, he found an inner calm and spiritual depth that he had not experienced through his religious upbringing. Meditation became his new spiritual practice, allowing him to maintain a sense of connection to something greater without adhering to the rules and rituals of his former faith.

2. Discussing Reasons for Leaving Organized Religion

Leaving organized religion is rarely a simple or impulsive decision. It is often the result of long-standing disillusionment, dissatisfaction with institutional practices, or a desire to live in a way that feels more authentic and aligned with one's personal values.

Disillusionment with Religious Institutions

A common reason for leaving organized religion is disillusionment with the institution itself. Many find themselves frustrated by the bureaucracy, hierarchy, or dogma that often defines religious organizations. Scandals, hypocrisy, or rigid rules can alienate believers, especially those who value personal spiritual freedom over strict adherence to doctrine.

- Frustration with Dogma and Hierarchy: Some individuals feel constrained by the rigid teachings or moral codes imposed by their religious institutions. For instance, a person might feel disconnected from a church that refuses to evolve on issues like gender equality or LGBTQ+ rights, sparking a desire to distance themselves from the institution and its limitations.

Personal Quest for Authenticity

Others leave organized religion because they are in search of something more personally meaningful. The rituals, doctrines, and belief systems that once provided comfort may begin to feel hollow or inauthentic. For these individuals, leaving religion is a way to embrace a more genuine, personal spiritual path that aligns with their own experiences and moral compass.

- Desire for a Genuine Spiritual Path: The quest for authenticity often arises when individuals feel that their spiritual life has become performative or disconnected from their inner sense of truth. They may desire a path that allows them to explore spirituality on their own terms, without the constraints of external rules or expectations.

3. Examining the Challenges of Leaving Religion

Leaving organized religion can be an emotionally and socially complex experience. It often involves significant challenges, including navigating the loss of community, family tensions, and the emotional void left by stepping away from a structured faith tradition.

Familial and Social Repercussions

For many, leaving religion means navigating the difficult terrain of family dynamics and social expectations. Religious communities often provide a deep sense of belonging and identity, and stepping away from that can lead to feelings of isolation, rejection, or tension with loved ones.

- Navigating Relationships Post Departure: Leaving a faith tradition can strain family and social relationships, especially in tight-knit religious communities. Individuals who depart from their religious upbringing may face judgment, disappointment, or ostracization from family members or close friends. They may have to learn how to redefine relationships with those who still adhere to the beliefs they have left behind.

Search for New Meaning

Once someone leaves an organized religion, they are often left with the task of filling the spiritual or existential void left by their departure. Many former believers experience a period of uncertainty or aimlessness as they seek new ways to find meaning, purpose, and community.

- Filling the Void Left by Organized Religion: Without the structure, rituals, and teachings of an organized religion, individuals may struggle to find new frameworks for understanding life's big questions. This can lead to feelings of loss or confusion as they seek to develop new spiritual practices or philosophical perspectives that resonate with their evolving beliefs.

4. Highlighting the Benefits of Spiritual Independence

Despite the challenges, leaving organized religion can be a deeply empowering and liberating experience. By stepping away from institutionalized faith, individuals gain the freedom to explore new spiritual paths, define their own beliefs, and live in alignment with their personal values.

Freedom from Dogma

One of the greatest benefits of leaving organized religion is the freedom to explore spirituality without the constraints of dogma or rigid teachings. Individuals who embrace spiritual independence often find that they are able to deepen their spiritual connection in ways that feel more authentic and meaningful to them.

- Embracing Personal Spiritual Exploration: Without the need to conform to a particular set of beliefs or practices, individuals are free to experiment with different forms of spirituality. This might include exploring meditation, mindfulness, nature-based practices, or secular philosophies that offer meaning and insight.

Empowerment Through Self-Discovery

Leaving organized religion can also lead to a profound sense of empowerment and self-discovery. Individuals who forge their own spiritual path often experience a renewed sense of autonomy, personal growth, and inner strength.

- The Autonomy of Defining One's Own Beliefs: By taking ownership of their spiritual journey, individuals are empowered to define their own beliefs, values, and practices. This autonomy allows for a more personalized and flexible approach to spirituality, one that is responsive to their unique experiences and needs.

Example:

A person who has left behind a strict religious upbringing may find empowerment in the freedom to create their own rituals, choose their own spiritual mentors, or adopt practices from multiple traditions that resonate with them. This freedom fosters a sense of spiritual ownership and personal growth, as they are no longer bound by external authorities or rigid doctrines.

The Path of Spiritual Independence

Leaving organized religion is a journey filled with challenges, but it can also offer immense rewards. By stepping away from the constraints of dogma and institutionalized faith, individuals have the opportunity to explore spirituality on their own terms, forge new paths of meaning, and discover a deeper sense of authenticity and empowerment. Whether they find solace in alternative spiritual practices or create their own unique belief systems, those who embrace spiritual independence often experience a profound sense of liberation, growth, and personal fulfillment.

1. Defining Your Spiritual Identity: Beyond Labels

- Encourage Introspection: Guide readers to explore their unique spiritual beliefs through self-reflection.

- Personal Reflection Exercises: Offer questions and prompts to help uncover core values and beliefs.

- Identifying Influences: Help readers recognize how past experiences and relationships have shaped their current spiritual outlook.

- Limitations of Traditional Labels: Acknowledge that existing religious labels often fail to capture individual spiritual nuances.

- Moving Beyond Binary Labels: Discuss the concept of a spectrum of spiritual identities rather than fixed categories.

- Cultural and Societal Expectations: Address how societal norms can affect spiritual self-expression.

- Crafting a Personal Spiritual Narrative: Encourage readers to document their spiritual journey.

- Journaling Key Spiritual Moments: Reflect on pivotal experiences that shaped their beliefs.

- Writing a Spiritual Mission Statement: Define a purpose or guiding principle that resonates with their evolving beliefs.

2. Creating Sacred Spaces: Personal and Communal Practices

- What Makes a Space Sacred: Explore the qualities that turn a physical or mental space into a sanctuary for reflection.

- Personal vs. Communal Sacred Spaces: Discuss the unique roles of personal reflection spaces versus shared spiritual gathering spaces.

- Elements of Sacred Spaces: Highlight symbols, objects, and the atmosphere that foster connection.

- Practical Advice for Designing Personal Sacred Spaces: Help readers create spaces that resonate with their spiritual practices.

- Choosing the Right Location: Discuss how to find areas conducive to tranquility and focus.

- Incorporating Meaningful Artifacts: Suggest personal items (photographs, religious objects) that hold deep meaning.

- Role of Communal Spaces: The importance of sharing spiritual experiences in community settings.

- Inclusive Sacred Spaces: Discuss the importance of designing spaces that welcome diverse traditions and beliefs.

- Innovative Sacred Spaces: Inspire readers to think creatively, using nature or virtual platforms to foster spiritual connection.

3. Incorporating Diverse Beliefs: A Holistic Approach

- Eclectic Spirituality: Explain the value of drawing on multiple traditions to enrich spiritual understanding.

- Finding Common Threads: Identify universal principles that resonate across various spiritual practices.

- The Benefits of Hybrid Rituals: Combining different spiritual elements to create a personal practice.

- Integrating Diverse Spiritual Traditions: Offer methods for thoughtfully blending teachings and practices from multiple sources.

- Hybrid Rituals: Give examples, such as combining yoga with Christian prayer or mindfulness with indigenous wisdom.

- Comparative Religion Studies: Encourage exploration of various traditions to find deeper meaning and insight.

- Challenges in Integration: Discuss potential obstacles, such as:

- Cultural Appropriation: Guide readers on how to respect the origins of practices while incorporating them.

- Balancing Coherence with Diversity: Offer advice on how to maintain a unified belief system amidst eclectic influences.

4. Embracing Spiritual Flexibility: Adapting Beliefs Over Time

- The Importance of Flexibility: Emphasize why spiritual adaptability is key to growth and resilience.

- Evolving Beliefs: Frame changing beliefs as a sign of personal development and deepening faith.

- Resilience Through Adaptation: Show how being open to change strengthens spiritual convictions.

- Strategies for Adapting Beliefs: Offer methods for revisiting and revising belief systems.

- Regular Reflection and Assessment: Encourage periodic reviews of one's spiritual beliefs to ensure they align with personal growth.

- Openness to New Experiences: Urge readers to let life experiences shape their spiritual journey.

- Addressing Fears of Change: Help readers overcome anxieties about evolving their beliefs.

- Instability Fears: Reassure readers that change does not diminish stability; rather, it builds resilience.

- Letting Go of Old Beliefs: Guide readers in gracefully releasing beliefs that no longer serve them.

- Examples of Spiritual Flexibility: Share inspiring stories of individuals who have embraced change in their spiritual lives.

This approach not only emphasizes the individuality of spiritual exploration but also provides a balance of introspection, guidance, and creative flexibility. It invites readers to take ownership of their beliefs, empowering them to grow and adapt as their understanding of the world and themselves evolves

5. Defining Your Spiritual Identity: Beyond Labels

This section aims to help readers explore their spiritual identity without being confined to rigid labels or definitions. It encourages deep self-reflection, the recognition of influences, and the crafting of a personal narrative that authentically captures one's beliefs.

Encouraging Introspection: Understanding Your Spiritual Self

At the core of spiritual identity lies self-awareness. Often, we adopt religious or spiritual beliefs without questioning their alignment with our deeper selves. To define a personal belief system, introspection is essential. By turning inward, readers can uncover what truly resonates with them.

- Guided Self-Reflection: Encourage readers to set aside time for focused reflection. Questions such as:

- What do I believe about the nature of existence, the universe, or a higher power?

- How do I experience or perceive spirituality in my everyday life?

- What values guide my decisions and interactions with others?

These questions can serve as entry points into deeper self-discovery, encouraging the articulation of one's spiritual identity.

Personal Reflection Exercises: Questions to Uncover Core Values and Beliefs

Providing exercises and prompts helps readers think critically about their beliefs. Here are a few examples of reflection activities:

1. Values Mapping:

- List five values that are most important to you. Do these values align with any religious or spiritual teachings? How have they shaped your actions and decisions?

2. Belief Audit:

- Make a list of beliefs you currently hold, whether spiritual or secular. Reflect on their origins: Did they come from childhood teachings, cultural expectations, or personal experience? Are these beliefs still meaningful to you, or do they need re-evaluation?

3. Spiritual Autobiography:

- Write a brief autobiography focused on spiritual milestones. What are the key moments, experiences, or teachings that have shaped your current beliefs?

These exercises guide readers to move beyond surface-level beliefs to uncover the deeper values that truly resonate with their spiritual identities.

6. Identifying Influences: Recognizing the Impact of Past Experiences on Current Beliefs

Many of our beliefs are influenced by childhood teachings, cultural traditions, and formative life experiences. Recognizing these influences allows readers to determine which beliefs still serve them and which no longer fit.

- Family and Upbringing: How did your family or community shape your spiritual understanding? Are there any teachings you've outgrown, or any lessons that still resonate deeply?

- Life Experiences: Reflect on events that shifted or challenged your beliefs. A significant loss, a personal triumph, or travel to unfamiliar cultures often prompts shifts in spiritual perspective.

- Cultural and Societal Expectations: Consider the role of social and cultural norms. How have these external forces shaped your sense of spirituality? Are you conforming to an expectation, or do your beliefs genuinely reflect your personal experiences?

Encouraging readers to question and trace the origins of their beliefs can help them discern which aspects of their spiritual identity are self-directed versus inherited or imposed by society.

7. Discussing the Limitations of Traditional Labels: Moving Beyond Binary Classifications

Traditional religious labels—such as Christian, Hindu, or atheist—can be helpful, but they are often limited in fully describing a person's spiritual complexity. Many people feel an affinity to more than one belief system or may reject all labels in favor of a personal, evolving belief system.

- The Spectrum of Spirituality: Spirituality doesn't have to fit into binary categories. Some people may practice aspects of multiple traditions, while others may feel connected to nature, the universe, or an undefined force.

- Example: Someone might attend church occasionally, practice yoga as a spiritual discipline, and incorporate mindfulness practices from Buddhism. Their spirituality defies easy labeling.

- The Fluidity of Belief: It's important to emphasize that spiritual identity can change over time. A person may start with strict adherence to a particular faith and later find value in exploring other spiritual traditions.

- Example: A former evangelical Christian may still cherish the values of love and compassion from their religious upbringing while integrating elements of meditation and mindfulness from other traditions.

By discussing the limitations of labels, readers can embrace a more nuanced understanding of their own beliefs, recognizing that they may not fit into neatly defined categories.

8. Crafting a Personal Spiritual Narrative: Telling Your Own Story

Encourage readers to take ownership of their spiritual journey by crafting a personal narrative. This involves documenting the key moments, beliefs, and values that shape their spirituality.

- Journaling Pivotal Spiritual Moments: Guide readers to reflect on and write about their significant spiritual experiences. This could include moments of doubt, revelations, personal crises, or encounters with other belief systems. Journaling allows readers to see patterns and connections they may not have noticed before.

- Questions to Consider:

- What was your earliest memory of feeling connected to something greater than yourself?

- Have you experienced a spiritual crisis or moment of doubt? How did it shape your beliefs?

- What teachings or philosophies have had the greatest impact on your spiritual life?

- Writing a Spiritual Mission Statement: This is a powerful way for readers to distill their beliefs into a guiding principle or mission. It helps define their spiritual purpose and gives direction.

- Example Statement: "My spiritual journey is centered on cultivating kindness, embracing curiosity, and finding peace through meditation and gratitude."

A mission statement need not be static; it can evolve as the individual's spiritual identity grows and changes over time.

9. Highlighting the Value of a Flexible Spiritual Identity

Finally, the spiritual journey should be adaptable. Encourage readers to embrace flexibility, allowing their beliefs to evolve as they learn, grow, and encounter new experiences.

- Allowing for Evolution: Spiritual identity is not fixed; it evolves with experience. Embrace the notion that it's okay to change your mind, question your beliefs, and adjust your practices.

- Balancing Stability with Exploration: While flexibility is essential, finding a balance between change and stability can help maintain a sense of groundedness during spiritual exploration.

By helping readers embrace spiritual flexibility, they can continue to grow and evolve, adapting their beliefs to their personal and spiritual development.

Exercises

Here are some exercises designed to guide readers through the process of defining their spiritual identity, facilitating introspection, and encouraging personal growth.

Values Mapping Exercise

This exercise helps readers identify their core values and examine how these align with their current spiritual beliefs.

Step-by-Step Guide:

1. List Your Core Values:

*   Write down the five values you hold most dear. These could include kindness, honesty, freedom, compassion, justice, or any other principles that guide your life.

2. Reflect on Origins:

*   Next to each value, note where you think this value came from. Did you learn it from your family, a religious tradition, a life experience, or personal reflection?

3. Spiritual Alignment:

*   For each value, ask yourself:

*   Does this value align with my current spiritual beliefs?

*   How does this value manifest in my spiritual or religious practices?

4. Actionable Insights:

*   Consider whether your current spiritual identity honors these values. Are there any gaps or conflicts between your values and your beliefs that need attention?

Example:

*   Value: Compassion Origin: Grew up seeing my parents helping others in the community. Spiritual Alignment: I feel connected to this value through mindfulness practices, which remind me to be present and empathetic toward others. Action: Incorporate more acts of service or compassion-based meditation into my routine.

2. Spiritual Autobiography

Writing a spiritual autobiography can help readers trace the significant moments that shaped their beliefs and values. This exercise provides clarity on their spiritual evolution.

Step-by-Step Guide:

1. Divide Life into Chapters:

- Divide your life into chapters or phases (e.g., childhood, adolescence, young adulthood, etc.).

2. Identify Pivotal Moments:

- In each chapter, write about a few key experiences that influenced your spiritual beliefs. Consider questions like:

- What were your early spiritual beliefs or practices?

- Did you ever face a moment of doubt or change in belief?

- How have major life events (e.g., loss, love, illness) impacted your spirituality?

3. Reflect on Transitions:

- For each chapter, reflect on how your spiritual beliefs evolved. Were there times when you felt disconnected from your faith? How did you navigate those moments?

4. Connect the Dots:

- Once your autobiography is written, look for patterns. What themes have consistently appeared? Are there any recurring struggles or revelations that inform your spiritual identity today?

Example Reflection:

- Childhood: I attended church regularly with my family, but my personal connection to faith was weak.

- Adolescence: After losing a close friend, I began questioning the nature of life and death, which led me to explore meditation and mindfulness.

- Young Adulthood: Studying philosophy in college introduced me to different worldviews, expanding my perspective and helping me move beyond dogmatic beliefs.

- Now: I feel more connected to spirituality through nature and daily practices like gratitude journaling.

3. Belief Audit

This exercise encourages readers to take stock of their current beliefs and explore how they've changed or evolved over time.

Step-by-Step Guide:

1. Create a Belief Inventory:

- Write down your current spiritual or religious beliefs. Try to be as specific as possible. For example:

- "I believe in a higher power."

- "I practice gratitude daily as a spiritual ritual."

- "I believe that karma impacts my life."

2. Explore Origins:

- Next to each belief, note where it originated. Was it something you were taught as a child, something you discovered on your own, or something you've adopted from another tradition?

3. Assess Current Relevance:

- Reflect on whether each belief still resonates with you. Ask:

- Does this belief still feel true to me?

- Has this belief evolved over time?

- How does this belief affect my daily life and actions?

4. Make Adjustments:

- After reviewing your beliefs, consider whether any need to be adjusted, deepened, or even released. Write down any changes you'd like to make in your spiritual practice or belief system.

Example:

- Belief: I believe in reincarnation.Origin: This belief came from my family's Buddhist background.Relevance: I'm no longer certain whether I believe in literal reincarnation, but I do find value in the idea that actions have consequences beyond this life.Adjustment: I will focus on how my actions impact the present moment rather than the idea of future lives.

4. Writing a Spiritual Mission Statement

This exercise helps readers define a clear purpose or direction for their spiritual journey. It's a powerful way to summarize what they stand for and where they are headed.

Step-by-Step Guide:

1. Reflect on Core Beliefs:

- Begin by reviewing your most important spiritual beliefs and values. These could come from previous exercises like the Belief Audit or Values Mapping.

2. Identify Your Purpose:

- Ask yourself:

- What is my primary goal in my spiritual journey?

- How do I want to contribute to the world, or what impact do I want my beliefs to have on myself and others?

3. Craft the Statement:

- Using your reflections, write a short and clear mission statement that sums up your spiritual identity. Keep it focused and meaningful, and avoid jargon.

4. Review and Revise:

- As you grow and evolve, revisit and revise your statement. It should remain dynamic, just like your spiritual identity.

Example Mission Statement:

- "My spiritual journey is dedicated to fostering compassion, mindfulness, and gratitude in everyday life. I seek to understand the deeper connections between all beings and cultivate peace within myself and others."

5. Guided Meditation: Exploring Spiritual Identity

This exercise invites readers to explore their spiritual identity through a guided meditation focused on self-discovery and inner wisdom.

Step-by-Step Guide:

1. Find a Quiet Space:

- Sit comfortably in a quiet place where you won't be disturbed.

2. Set an Intention:

- Close your eyes and set the intention to explore your spiritual identity. You might say, "I am open to discovering what truly resonates with me spiritually."

3. Deep Breathing:

- Focus on your breath for a few minutes, allowing your body to relax and your mind to calm down.

4. Visualization:

- Imagine you are walking on a path that represents your spiritual journey. Along the way, you encounter symbols, people, or experiences that have shaped your beliefs. Take note of these symbols and what they mean to you.

5. Ask for Insight:

- In your meditation, ask, "What is my true spiritual path?" Allow any feelings, images, or thoughts to arise without judgment.

6. Journal Afterward:

- Once the meditation is complete, take a few minutes to journal about what came up. Did any insights or realizations emerge about your spiritual identity?

6. Letting Go with Gratitude

For those who are moving away from old beliefs, this exercise offers a compassionate way to let go of beliefs that no longer serve them while acknowledging the value they once had.

Step-by-Step Guide:

1. Identify a Belief to Release:

- Think of a belief or spiritual practice that no longer resonates with you. Write it down.

2. Acknowledge Its Purpose:

- Reflect on the role this belief played in your life. How did it serve you in the past? What lessons did it teach you?

3. Express Gratitude:

- Write a note of gratitude to the belief. For example: "Thank you for helping me find comfort during difficult times. I now release you with gratitude, as you no longer align with who I am becoming."

4. Release the Belief:

- Perform a symbolic action to let go of the belief. You could burn the piece of paper where you wrote the belief, tear it up, or simply set it aside with intention.

5. Journal About the Process:

- Write about how it feels to let go. What new space or possibilities does this create for you?

These exercises encourage self-exploration, reflection, and active engagement in shaping one's spiritual identity. They are designed to be adaptable and can be repeated as needed, allowing for continual spiritual growth and evolution.

CHAPTER 4

PHILOSOPHICAL AND INTELLECTUAL EXPLORATION: MORAL DILEMMAS WITHIN FAITH

4.1 The Complexity of Moral Decision-Making

Faith-based moral frameworks often provide clear guidance, but real-life situations can create ethical dilemmas. For instance, the ethics of war in Christianity poses questions about when, if ever, it is permissible to take life. The "Just War Theory" offers principles like legitimate authority and proportionality, but modern conflicts often blur these lines, creating moral uncertainty.

Example: Ethical Decisions in Religious Contexts

The Ethics of War in Christianity:

Christianity teaches love and peace, but historical contexts, such as medieval crusades or World War II, have seen moral arguments made for war. How can religious leaders reconcile these contradictions?

- **Case Study: Forgiveness versus Justice**

Faith traditions emphasize forgiveness in situations of harm or crime, but justice is also a strong tenet. The debate between forgiving an offender and seeking justice, especially in cases like violent crime, reflects the moral complexity inherent in religious teachings. For example, should a victim's family forgive a murderer, as taught in Christianity, or pursue justice through the legal system?

Interpreting Sacred Texts for Moral Guidance

Sacred texts serve as primary sources for moral decision-making, but interpretations can vary widely, leading to different ethical conclusions.

- **Comparative Analysis of Interpretations of the Quran on Societal Issues**

Islamic scholars interpret the Quran's teachings on societal roles, gender, and justice in varied ways. Interpretations of specific verses often shape debates on women's rights in Muslim societies. Yet, progressive movements within Islam advocate for gender equality based on other readings of the same texts.

The Role of Rabbinic Commentary in Jewish Ethical Decision-Making

In Judaism, rabbinic commentary plays a crucial role in ethical discussions. The Talmud and later rabbinical writings often offer nuanced interpretations of Torah laws, helping practitioners navigate modern moral issues like technology, bioethics, and business ethics. For example, ethical questions regarding the use of AI in Jewish law are being explored through the lens of ancient rabbinic debates on human responsibility.

Personal versus Collective Morality

There is often a tension between individual moral beliefs and the collective moral stance of a religious community. While religious institutions may hold particular views, individuals within those communities may challenge or reinterpret these teachings based on personal experiences or evolving social norms.

- **Stories of Individuals Challenging Their Community's Moral Stance**

Many individuals confront conflicts between their personal morality and the collective teachings of their faith. Consider the story of a Catholic woman advocating for reproductive rights, even though her church condemns contraception and abortion. Her decision to challenge the church's teachings reflects a deeply personal moral exploration that may clash with collective religious norms.

- **The Impact of Cultural Context on Collective Religious Morality**

Religious teachings don't exist in a vacuum; they evolve within cultural contexts. For example, collective morality in some religious communities may shift when they migrate to a new country, adapting to the surrounding cultural norms, as seen in progressive Christian churches embracing LGBTQ+ rights in the West despite more traditional views elsewhere.

Evolving Moral Codes in Modern Faiths

As society confronts new ethical challenges, traditional religious moral codes often need to adapt.

- **Climate Change Ethics in Contemporary Religious Thought**

Many religious traditions, from Christianity to Buddhism, are reinterpreting their teachings to address climate change. Pope Francis' encyclical Laudato Si' emphasizes environmental stewardship, framing it as a moral responsibility. In Buddhism, the concept of ahimsa (non-harm) is being applied to climate action, urging practitioners to reduce their carbon footprint.

- **The Role of Feminist Theology in Reshaping Religious Moral Teachings**

Feminist theologians in Christianity, Islam, and Judaism are reinterpreting religious texts to promote gender equality. They argue that patriarchal interpretations have shaped much of religious history and advocate for more inclusive moral frameworks, such as rethinking women's roles in leadership within these faiths.

4.2 Philosophical Debates on Divine Existence

Arguments for and Against Divine Existence

- **The Ontological Argument and Its Critiques**

The ontological argument, first posited by St. Anselm, suggests that God must exist because He is the greatest conceivable being, and a being that exists is greater than one that doesn't. Critics like Immanuel Kant, however, argue that existence is not a predicate, and therefore, the argument fails.

- **Modern Atheistic Perspectives and the Problem of Evil**

Modern atheists, like Richard Dawkins, argue against the existence of God based on the problem of evil—how can an all-good, all-powerful God allow suffering? The tension between divine omnipotence and the existence of evil remains a central philosophical dilemma.

The Role of Faith in Philosophical Inquiry

Philosophical inquiry often grapples with questions of faith. Faith and reason are not always at odds but can pose significant tensions.

- **Kierkegaard's Leap of Faith**

Søren Kierkegaard's philosophy suggests that religious belief is not based on rational evidence but a "leap of faith." He contrasts this with the rationalist's demand for proof, arguing that true belief involves embracing the uncertainty and risks associated with faith.

- **Rationalist versus Fideist Approaches to Belief**

Rationalists like Thomas Aquinas seek to harmonize reason and faith, using philosophical arguments to support religious doctrines. Fideists, by contrast, assert that faith transcends reason and should not be subject to rational proof, focusing on personal trust in the divine rather than intellectual evidence.

Philosophers Who Influenced Religious Thought

- **The Influence of Aristotle on Medieval Islamic Philosophy**

Aristotle's works shaped medieval Islamic philosophy, especially through figures like Avicenna (Ibn Sina) and Averroes (Ibn Rushd). They sought to reconcile Greek philosophy with Islamic teachings, influencing both Islamic and Western Christian thought.

- **Contributions of Descartes to Christian Theological Debates**

René Descartes, known for his philosophy of dualism (mind and body), also contributed to Christian theology by arguing for the existence of God through his famous "cogito, ergo sum" reasoning. His arguments have shaped modern debates on the nature of the soul and consciousness within Christian thought.

4.3 Exploring Secular Ethics and Spiritual Morality

Secular Moral Philosophies

Secular ethical frameworks like utilitarianism focus on maximizing well-being without invoking religious teachings. Utilitarianism, for instance, weighs the moral worth of an action based on its consequences, promoting the greatest good for the greatest number.

Spirituality Beyond Religion

Many individuals find moral guidance in spirituality outside of traditional religion, such as through mindfulness and meditation practices. These often emphasize inner peace, compassion, and ethical living without adhering to specific religious dogmas.

Reconciling Secular and Religious Morality

Interfaith families and individuals navigating both secular and religious beliefs often engage in ongoing dialogue to reconcile these two frameworks. Many find common ethical principles, such as compassion or justice, that transcend the divide between secularism and religion.

This exploration demonstrates the depth and variety in how moral and philosophical questions are navigated within and beyond faith traditions. These complex issues often lead individuals to reevaluate their beliefs and understanding of morality, leading to personal and communal growth.

CHAPTER 5

PRACTICAL GUIDANCE FOR NAVIGATING DOUBT

In the dim light of early morning, I found myself seated at my desk, a blank journal open before me. The quiet of the hour offered a sanctuary from the chaos of daily life, providing a moment of introspection that seemed to beckon the soul. As the pen touched the paper, thoughts began to flow, unfiltered and raw. Writing has always been a refuge, a space where the complexities of the heart and mind can find clarity. Journaling, in particular, is a powerful tool for navigating the turbulent waters of doubt. It allows you to explore your inner landscape, unraveling the knots of confusion and uncertainty that often accompany spiritual questioning.

Journaling offers a structured approach to self-reflection, guiding you through the labyrinth of your thoughts and feelings. By engaging in this practice, you create a dialogue with yourself, where questions can be asked and answers gradually revealed. Structured journaling prompts can be particularly helpful in focusing your reflections. Questions such as "What are my deepest doubts?" or "How do these doubts affect my sense of self?" encourage you to delve deeper into the roots of your uncertainty. On the other hand, free writing exercises invite you to let your thoughts flow without restraint, capturing the nuances of your fears and uncertainties. This process of uncensored expression can be liberating, allowing you to confront and articulate the aspects of doubt that may have remained hidden.

The benefits of journaling extend beyond mere expression; they offer profound insights and personal growth. Regular journaling creates a record of your journey, allowing you to track patterns and identify the triggers of recurring doubts. By examining these patterns, you gain a clearer understanding of the underlying causes of your uncertainty, enabling you to address them more effectively. The act of writing itself is cathartic, providing an emotional release that can alleviate the weight of unspoken fears. As you pour your thoughts onto the page, you create a space for healing and renewal, transforming turmoil into clarity and peace.

Consistency is critical to maximizing the impact of journaling on your spiritual exploration. Setting a regular journaling schedule helps establish a routine, making it an integral part of your daily practice. Whether you write in the morning, when your mind is fresh or in the evening, when the events of the day can be reflected upon, consistency fosters a sense of commitment to your growth.

Integrating journaling with other reflective practices, such as meditation or prayer, can deepen your insights. Combining these practices creates a holistic approach to self-discovery, where mind, body, and spirit align in the pursuit of understanding.

The catalyzing power of journaling is evident in the stories of those who have embraced this practice. Consider the experience of a young woman who, feeling lost and disconnected from her faith, began journaling each evening. Through her writing, she unearthed fears that had long been buried, allowing her to confront and release them. Over time, her journal became a testament to her resilience, a record of her journey from doubt to clarity. Another individual, grappling with a crisis of belief, found solace in the pages of his journal. As he wrote, he discovered patterns in his thinking that had previously eluded him, leading to breakthroughs that reshaped his understanding of faith.

Reflection Exercise: Journaling for Clarity

- Begin with a Prompt: To guide your reflection, choose a question such as "What is the source of my doubts?"

- Allow Free Expression: Set a timer for 10 minutes and write without stopping. Let your thoughts flow freely, capturing whatever arises.

- Reflect on Patterns: Review your entries after a week, looking for recurring, emerging themes or insights.

In its quiet simplicity, journaling offers a powerful means of navigating doubt and providing clarity and insight into one's spiritual path.

5.1 Mindfulness Practices: Grounding the Spirit

In the hustle and bustle of daily life, doubt often sneaks in, whispering uncertainty into the quiet corners of your mind. It tends to amplify fears and obscure clarity, making mindfulness a crucial ally in managing these feelings. Mindfulness, the practice of staying present, invites you to anchor your awareness in the now, where past regrets and future worries lose their hold. Focusing on the present moment creates a sanctuary of calm amidst the chaos. This isn't just about sitting in silence; it's an active engagement with your surroundings and your inner world. Techniques such as paying attention to the rhythm of your breath or noticing the sensations in your body can ground you, offering a respite from the spiral of anxious thoughts.

Breathing exercises are a gateway to mindfulness, providing a simple yet profound way to calm the mind and body. With each inhale and exhale, you draw your attention away from cluttered thoughts and toward your breath's steady, life-giving force. Though deceptively simple, this practice can create space between you and your reactions, allowing you to approach doubt with a sense of peace. Picture yourself sitting comfortably, eyes gently closed, as you breathe in deeply, feeling your chest rise, then exhale slowly, releasing tension with each breath. This rhythmic focus centers your mind, reducing anxiety and fostering a sense of balance.

Mindfulness offers more than just a temporary escape from stress—it fosters a deeper connection with your inner self. As you practice mindfulness regularly, you cultivate enhanced self-awareness, recognizing and accepting thoughts and feelings without judgment. This acceptance is transformative; it allows you to see your doubts not as threats but as natural aspects of your human experience. When you acknowledge your thoughts without attaching to them, you free yourself from the cycle of criticism and fear. The reduction in stress that accompanies mindfulness practice emerges as you build this habit. Over time, you may find that the ever-present weight of doubt begins to lift, replaced by a tranquility that comes from engaging fully with the present.

Integrating mindfulness into your spiritual growth involves specific practices that align with your journey. Mindful meditation is one such technique, encouraging you to observe your thoughts as they arise, letting them pass like clouds in the sky. This practice teaches you to witness your mental chatter without becoming entangled in it, fostering a sense of detachment and clarity. Body scan exercises offer another avenue for connection, guiding you to focus on each part of your body and recognize physical sensations and their links to emotional states. Through these scans, you develop a holistic awareness of your being, weaving a tapestry of physical and spiritual understanding.

Countless stories of transformation illustrate the impact of mindfulness on spiritual exploration. Consider the experience of a man who, overwhelmed by doubts, turned to mindfulness to find peace. Through consistent practice, he discovered a newfound clarity, his anxieties gradually replaced by a sense of calm. Once fraught with tension, his spiritual practices became opportunities for connection and insight. Another individual, struggling with the stress of uncertainty, found that mindfulness reduced her anxiety, allowing her to embrace her spiritual path with openness and curiosity. These examples highlight the potential of mindfulness to guide you through doubt, offering not just relief but a path toward deeper understanding and spiritual fulfillment.

5.2 Engaging in Open Dialogue: Conversations That Heal

There's a profound comfort that arises when you share your innermost thoughts with someone who listens without judgment. In moments of doubt, conversations can illuminate paths you hadn't considered, offering new perspectives and emotional support. Engaging in open dialogue is more than just talking; it's about creating a space where words are safe and your thoughts and feelings can be laid bare without fear of ridicule or dismissal. Empathy plays a pivotal role in these exchanges. It allows for listening that goes beyond just hearing words. It's about hearing the emotion behind those words and responding with genuine understanding. When someone listens empathetically, it feels like an embrace, a recognition that your experiences matter.

Creating safe spaces for discussion is fundamental in fostering these healing dialogues. Setting boundaries and fostering trust are essential steps in this process. Trust is the foundation upon which meaningful conversation is built. Without it, words may feel hollow, and honesty becomes a risk rather than a release. Safe spaces are those rare environments where openness is encouraged and respected. They are cultivated through mutual respect and a shared commitment to understanding, where each participant feels valued and heard. In these spaces, you can express your doubts openly, knowing your vulnerability will be met with support rather than judgment. They are sanctuaries where the sacredness of dialogue is honored, providing a refuge from the noise of everyday life.

Sharing your doubts with others validates your feelings and can lead to fresh insights. When you articulate your questions and uncertainties, you often find clarity in the mere act of speaking them aloud. In dialogue, you gain access to new perspectives, learning from others' experiences and viewpoints. These conversations can be enlightening, revealing aspects of your doubts that you might not have seen on your own. They offer a mirror, reflecting back your own thoughts in the light of someone else's understanding. Moreover, feeling heard and understood provides emotional validation. When someone acknowledges your struggles without trying to fix them, it affirms your right to feel what you feel. This validation can be incredibly healing, reinforcing the notion that you are not alone in your uncertainty.

Engaging in effective dialogue requires specific skills and strategies. Active listening is paramount. This involves focusing on understanding rather than immediately responding. It means giving your full attention, putting aside preconceived notions, and genuinely absorbing what the other person is saying. Questioning frameworks that encourage open-ended, exploratory questions can also guide these conversations. Such questions invite deeper reflection and help uncover underlying issues. They are gentle prompts that nudge the conversation toward discovery rather than debate. Approaching dialogue with curiosity rather than judgment opens the door to meaningful exchange, allowing both parties to explore their thoughts and feelings without the pressure to defend or convince.

The life-changing power of dialogue is evident in countless stories of healing and growth. Consider the case of an interfaith dialogue group where individuals from different religious backgrounds came together to share their stories. They discovered common ground through these conversations, fostering mutual understanding and respect. The dialogues allowed them to see beyond their differences, focusing instead on shared values and experiences. In another instance, a person struggling with doubts about their spiritual path found solace in community discussions. Through open dialogue, they realized that many others shared similar struggles, leading to a sense of belonging and support. These examples highlight how conversation can bridge divides, offering comfort and clarity to those navigating the complexities of faith and doubt.

5.3 Seeking Reliable Guidance: Identifying Trustworthy Sources

In the labyrinth of spiritual exploration, finding reliable guidance is like discovering a lighthouse in the fog. It provides direction and clarity, helping you navigate the complex terrain of doubt and belief. The path of spiritual inquiry is fraught with potential pitfalls, particularly the risk of misinformation. In an age where information is readily accessible and opinions masquerading as facts, relying on unreliable or biased sources can lead you astray, sowing confusion instead of clarity. Misleading guidance can distort your understanding, creating barriers to genuine exploration and growth. This underscores the necessity of seeking out credible mentors who offer wisdom rooted in knowledge and empathy. Such individuals do not merely provide answers; they guide you to ask the right questions, fostering an environment where your spiritual doubts can be explored without judgment.

To discern trustworthy sources, it's crucial to have a framework for evaluating their credibility. Start by examining the credentials and experience of those offering guidance. Are they well-versed in the areas they claim expertise in? Do they have a history of thoughtful engagement with spiritual topics? These questions help ascertain the depth of their understanding. Equally important is assessing their transparency and openness. Reliable guides encourage exploration, welcoming questions and fostering dialogue. They do not shy away from admitting what they do not know, valuing the journey of discovery over the pretense of certainty.

Trustworthy sources are those who provide space for your voice, encouraging you to think critically and form your own conclusions.

Connecting with reliable mentors or resources requires proactive strategies. One effective approach is networking within spiritual communities. These communities often host individuals who have walked similar paths, possessing insights and experiences that can illuminate your own. Engaging with these groups allows you to build connections and identify mentors whose guidance resonates with you. Additionally, the vast digital landscape offers a plethora of resources, but it is essential to carefully research and vet online content. Evaluate the credibility of digital sources by considering their authorship, the evidence supporting their claims, and the balance of perspectives they present. A thoughtful examination of online materials helps distinguish between superficial content and genuinely insightful resources.

The impact of reliable guidance is vividly illustrated in the stories of those who have found clarity through mentorship. Take the example of a young man, adrift in a sea of spiritual uncertainty, who found a mentor through his local community group. This mentor, a seasoned spiritual teacher, provided a safe space for inquiry, listening attentively and offering wisdom without imposing beliefs. Through their conversations, the young man discovered a renewed sense of direction; his doubts transformed into stepping stones on a path of personal growth. Similarly, consider the testimony of an individual who, after extensive research, found solace in an online community dedicated to thoughtful religious discussion. The balanced perspectives shared in this digital space offered insights that led to profound spiritual breakthroughs, helping her navigate her doubts with newfound confidence.

These narratives highlight the profound influence of reliable guidance on spiritual exploration. Trustworthy sources do not dictate the path; they illuminate it, ensuring that your journey is one of authentic discovery. As you seek out mentors and resources, remember that the goal is not to find definitive answers but to engage in a process that deepens your understanding and enriches your spiritual life. In the next chapter, we will explore the process of reconstructing faith, offering tools and perspectives to help you build a personal belief system that resonates with your unique experiences and insights.

CHAPTER 6

EMPATHY AND UNDERSTANDING IN FAITH DISCUSSIONS

In the hushed moments before dawn, I found myself seated at a kitchen table, the aroma of freshly brewed coffee mingling with the morning air. Across from me was my old friend, someone whose life had been shaped by beliefs different from mine. As we spoke, the conversation naturally drifted toward faith. I realized that listening, truly listening, was more than just hearing words. It was about opening a space for understanding, allowing each word to resonate with the heart. This exchange was a reminder of the profound power of compassionate listening—a practice that transcends mere dialogue and transforms interactions into moments of profound connection.

To engage with diverse viewpoints, one must first embrace the art of compassionate listening. This involves connecting with others by focusing on their needs and offering them patience and kindness. You listen not only with your ears but with your entire being, creating a channel for empathy to flow. Compassionate listening is an act of love that aligns with the mindset of Christ, an essential practice in Christian fellowship. When you listen without judgment, you validate the speaker's experience, fostering a sense of safety and trust. This kind of listening is not passive; it requires active engagement, where you genuinely seek to understand and share in the speaker's thoughts and feelings. Reflective listening, a key component of this practice, involves paraphrasing and reflecting back what is heard. It ensures that both the speaker and listener are on the same page, confirming that the message has been accurately received and understood.

The impact of compassionate listening on dialogue cannot be overstated. When approached with empathy, conversations have the potential to break down barriers and build bridges. Listening attentively can reduce defensiveness, allowing individuals to feel heard and respected. This shift in dynamics opens the door to more honest and open communication, where ideas can be shared without fear of judgment. As trust is established through attentive engagement, relationships deepen, and understanding flourishes. Proverbs 20:5 suggests that understanding others' deep feelings and thoughts requires effort and empathy, a sentiment that underscores the transformative power of compassionate listening. It is through this process that dialogue becomes a means of bearing one another's burdens, offering comfort and grace.

Developing listening skills is a journey that involves practice and reflection. Role-playing scenarios offer an opportunity to practice active listening in controlled settings, where you can hone your ability to genuinely hear and understand others. These exercises encourage you to focus on the speaker, minimizing distractions and engaging with their story. Journaling reflections is another valuable tool. By writing about your listening experiences, you can gain insights into your strengths and areas for improvement. This process allows you to reflect on how your listening has impacted your interactions and relationships, offering a road map for growth and development.

Stories of successful, compassionate dialogue abound, offering inspiration and guidance. Consider the faith leader who mediated a community dispute through empathetic listening. By creating a space where each party felt heard and valued, the leader was able to facilitate a resolution that honored the concerns of all involved. Personal testimonies reveal how listening with empathy can change perspectives, leading to understanding and healing. These narratives highlight the potential for compassionate listening to transform individual interactions and entire communities, fostering an environment of respect and collaboration.

In this chapter, I invite you to explore the practice of compassionate listening and consider how it can enrich your own faith discussions. Whether engaging with friends, family, or strangers, listen with an open heart and mind. Embrace the opportunity to connect on a deeper level, recognizing that each conversation holds the potential for growth and understanding. Through compassionate listening, we can create a world where empathy and love guide our interactions, bridging divides and nurturing the bonds that unite us.

6.1 Respecting Differences: Building Interfaith Bridges

In an increasingly interconnected world, respecting differences is not just a nicety but a necessity. Acknowledging and valuing diversity in interfaith interactions is crucial for fostering genuine understanding. It is through this lens of respect that we begin to see the beauty in our differences rather than perceiving them as obstacles. Cultural sensitivity plays a pivotal role here. It requires us to understand and respect cultural nuances and to approach each interaction with an open mind and a willingness to learn. This sensitivity allows for a richer, more authentic dialogue where each person's background and beliefs are honored. Humility is equally important, as it encourages us to approach discussions without the need to dominate or impose our views. It prompts us to listen and understand rather than simply wait for our turn to speak. This humility builds a foundation of mutual respect, where all voices are valued and heard.

Connecting with and appreciating different faith traditions is an endeavor that requires intentionality and effort. One effective method is participating in interfaith dialogue events. These gatherings offer a platform for individuals from diverse backgrounds to come together, share their beliefs, and explore common ground. These events can take many forms, from formal discussions to casual meet-ups, but they all aim to foster understanding and empathy. Collaborative community service projects are another powerful way to build interfaith bridges. By working together for common causes, individuals from different faiths can unite in their shared humanity, transcending doctrinal differences. These projects not only address tangible needs in the community but also create opportunities for meaningful connections and friendships. Through shared efforts and goals, participants are reminded that despite their differences, they are working toward a common good.

However, building interfaith bridges is not without its challenges. Overcoming prejudice is a significant hurdle, as biases and stereotypes can cloud our judgment and hinder genuine connection. Addressing these biases requires intentional self-reflection and a commitment to challenge preconceived notions. It involves looking beyond surface-level differences to see the individual, recognizing that each person is more than the labels society has assigned them. Navigating theological disagreements can also be challenging, as deeply held beliefs may seem incompatible at first glance. Yet, finding common ground amidst these differences is possible and often rewarding. It requires patience, open-mindedness, and a willingness to engage in honest and respectful dialogue. Through these conversations, we can learn to appreciate the richness of diverse perspectives, finding points of connection even in disagreement.

Successful interfaith initiatives provide inspiration and guidance for those seeking to bridge divides. Consider an interreligious council in a diverse city that promotes peace and understanding. This council, composed of leaders from various religious backgrounds, works collaboratively to address community issues, demonstrating the power of unity in diversity. Through regular meetings and public forums, they create spaces for dialogue, education, and collaboration, fostering a sense of community that transcends religious boundaries. Another example is a community festival that celebrates multiple spiritual traditions. This festival invites individuals from all backgrounds to participate in cultural exchanges, share their traditions, and engage in open dialogue. Such events highlight the beauty of diversity, offering a tangible reminder that our differences can be a source of strength and connection. These initiatives serve as beacons of hope, illustrating what is possible when we come together with respect and understanding. They remind us that, despite the challenges, building interfaith bridges is both necessary and profoundly rewarding.

6.2 The Power of Storytelling: Sharing and Receiving Faith Narratives

Sitting around a crackling campfire, you might find yourself drawn into the world of the storyteller, captivated by the tales that unfold. This ancient practice of storytelling is not merely an exchange of words; it is a bridge between hearts, a way to connect with others on a profound level. Sharing personal narratives has the power to transcend cultural and religious divides, resonating with core human experiences that are universal. Stories are more than just entertainment; they are vessels of empathy and understanding, capable of healing wounds and mending rifts. When you share your story, you offer a glimpse into your soul, inviting others to walk alongside you, even if just for a moment. This act of vulnerability can be transformative, not only for the teller but also for the listener. It is through these shared narratives that you process and overcome trauma, finding solace in the knowledge that you are not alone.

Crafting and sharing compelling faith narratives requires intention and skill. At the heart of every good story is a structure—

a beginning that draws in the listener, a middle that delves into the heart of the matter, and an end that leaves a lasting impression. This structure provides a roadmap for the journey you wish to take your audience on, guiding them through the peaks and valleys of your experience. To truly engage your listeners, use sensory details that bring your story to life. Describe the vivid colors of a sunset that marked a moment of revelation or the sound of rain tapping against the window during a night of doubt. These details create an immersive experience, allowing your audience to see, hear, and feel the world as you do. By painting a picture with words, you invite others into your narrative, helping them to understand and empathize with your journey.

Listening plays a crucial role in storytelling, transforming the exchange into a dialogue rather than a monologue. When you receive stories with openness and empathy, you create a safe environment where storytellers feel respected and heard. Demonstrating attentiveness through non-verbal cues, such as nodding or maintaining eye contact, signals to the speaker that you are fully present and engaged. Your body language can convey understanding and support, encouraging the storyteller to share more deeply. Creating a space where individuals feel safe to express their truths is essential for genuine connection. When storytellers know they are being heard without judgment, they are more likely to open up, enriching the experience for both parties.

Consider the impact of a faith-sharing circle, where individuals from diverse backgrounds come together to share their personal stories. In this space, each person has the opportunity to speak their truth, knowing that they are surrounded by others who are committed to listening with empathy. These circles are not just about sharing experiences; they are about creating a community built on mutual respect and understanding. Similarly, a storytelling event can unite a community after a divisive incident, offering a platform for healing and reconciliation. During such an event, people are invited to share narratives that highlight common values and shared humanity, reminding the audience of their interconnectedness. These stories have the power to transcend differences, fostering a sense of unity and solidarity that can pave the way for lasting change.

Storytelling is a powerful tool in faith discussions, offering a pathway to bridge divides and foster empathy. By sharing and receiving narratives with openness and respect, you can connect with others on a deeper level, creating a tapestry of understanding that enriches both the individual and the community.

6.3 Healing Divides: Creating Inclusive Spiritual Spaces

In the quiet of a Sunday evening, as the sun dips below the horizon, one might find solace in a place where all are welcome. These inclusive spiritual spaces are more than just physical structures; they are sanctuaries where diversity is celebrated and everyone feels valued. The essence of inclusivity lies in its ability to heal divides, offering a warm embrace to those who have often felt marginalized or unseen. By creating environments that welcome all walks of life, we foster a sense of community well-being and cohesion, breaking down barriers that have long kept people apart. Inclusivity is characterized by openness, where differences are acknowledged and respected, and each person's unique spiritual journey is honored. In these spaces, the walls echo with the voices of many, each contributing to a harmonious tapestry of beliefs and practices.

To cultivate such inclusive environments, we must be intentional in our efforts. It begins with the language we use, ensuring it communicates respect for all identities. Inclusive language is not merely about avoiding exclusionary terms but about actively inviting everyone into the conversation. It means being mindful of how words can uplift or diminish, creating a welcoming and affirming dialogue. Equally important is the consideration of universal design principles, which ensure that spiritual spaces are physically accessible to all. This means accommodating those with disabilities through ramps, hearing aids, or other necessary modifications so that everyone can participate fully in communal activities. Such considerations demonstrate a commitment to inclusivity, signaling that no one is left on the outside looking in.

Despite the best intentions, creating inclusive spaces is not without its challenges. Resistance to change is a common barrier as individuals and communities grapple with the discomfort of shifting long-held practices. Overcoming this reluctance requires patience, persistence, and clear communication about the benefits of inclusivity. Engaging community members in the process, inviting their input, and addressing concerns can help ease the transition. Another significant challenge is addressing biases that might exist within the community. Training and education for leaders and members can shed light on unconscious prejudices, equipping them with the tools to foster a more inclusive environment. By confronting these biases head-on, communities can begin to transform, opening themselves to a richer and more diverse faith experience.

Examples of communities that have successfully embraced inclusivity abound, offering inspiration and practical models for others to follow. Take, for instance, a church that has implemented programs designed explicitly for marginalized groups. By providing resources and support tailored to their needs, the church not only welcomes these individuals but actively affirms their place within the community. Such programs might include support groups for LGBTQ+ individuals, workshops on cultural sensitivity, or outreach initiatives aimed at economically disadvantaged populations. These efforts not only enrich the community but also serve as a testament to the church's commitment to inclusivity.

Similarly, a spiritual retreat center that opens its doors to individuals of all backgrounds showcases the power of inclusivity in action. By creating an environment where diverse traditions are not only accepted but celebrated, the center becomes a beacon of unity and understanding. Visitors might partake in various spiritual practices, from meditation and yoga to prayer and reflection, each finding a space that resonates with their beliefs. Through shared meals, discussions, and activities, individuals from different backgrounds connect, fostering a sense of belonging and mutual respect. Such examples illustrate that inclusivity is not just an ideal but a tangible reality that can transform communities and individuals alike. These spaces, where everyone is welcome and valued, remind us of the potential for healing and growth when we embrace diversity and inclusivity. They serve as models for what is possible when we commit to creating environments that honor and celebrate the richness of human experience.

In a sunlit room filled with the hum of conversation, I was drawn into a lively debate on gender roles within religious traditions. The discussion was sparked by a friend's casual remark about how her grandmother had been the backbone of their church, a silent leader who never claimed the pulpit. This conversation illuminated the invisible threads that have long woven traditional gender roles into the fabric of religious life. For centuries, many faiths have delineated specific roles for men and women, often dictated by cultural norms intertwined with sacred texts. In Christianity, interpretations of biblical passages have historically positioned men as leaders and women as supporters, a dynamic echoed in many religious teachings worldwide. Similarly, Bible verses advocate for the earth's care. These roles, interpreted in diverse ways across cultures, Islamic teachings have often emphasized distinct roles for men and women, shaping societal expectations. While roles provide structure, there are also limited opportunities for many, particularly women, to participate fully in spiritual leadership.

Feminist theology, a movement seeking equality within religious contexts, challenges these historical interpretations. By employing feminist methodologies, scholars and theologians advocate for a reexamination of sacred texts, questioning traditional narratives and proposing more inclusive readings (SOURCE 1). This approach often involves a "hermeneutic of suspicion," where traditional interpretations are scrutinized for biases that may have arisen from patriarchal influences. Feminist theologians argue that male-dominated readings of religious texts have historically marginalized women's voices, shaping doctrines that reinforce gender inequality. By highlighting the value of women's experiences and contributions, feminist theology calls for a broader understanding of spiritual narratives that reflect the diverse realities of all believers.

The influence of feminist theology extends beyond academic circles, impacting religious communities globally. Across traditions, women are increasingly assuming leadership roles, challenging longstanding norms. In Christianity, numerous denominations now ordain female clergy, recognizing their capacity to lead and inspire congregations. This shift signifies a broader movement towards gender equality within religious institutions, aligning with contemporary values of inclusivity and justice. In Islam, feminist movements advocate for women's rights within the framework of faith, striving for interpretations that honor women's contributions to religious life. These movements are often spearheaded by women who blend traditional Islamic teachings with contemporary understandings of gender equality, seeking to harmonize faith with the realities of modern life.

Gender equality movements have profoundly impacted religious doctrines and practices, prompting a reevaluation of traditional roles. Egalitarian movements within various faiths emphasize shared responsibilities and leadership opportunities for all, regardless of gender. These initiatives challenge the status quo, advocating for changes in policy and practice to reflect a commitment to equality. As religious groups embrace these principles, they often revisit doctrines that once reinforced gender hierarchies, seeking interpretations that affirm the dignity and potential of every individual. This transformation is not without resistance, as deeply ingrained beliefs can be slow to change. Yet, the momentum towards inclusivity reflects a growing recognition of the need for faith communities to evolve alongside societal shifts.

Consider the examples of religious communities that have successfully adapted to modern gender perspectives. A Christian denomination's decision to ordain female clergy marked a significant departure from tradition, opening doors for women to serve as spiritual leaders. This change was driven by a recognition of women's contributions to the faith and a desire to reflect contemporary values of equality. Similarly, Islamic feminist movements advocate for women's rights within religious frameworks, challenging interpretations that have historically limited their participation. These movements often emphasize the compatibility of gender equality with Islamic principles, seeking to empower women within their communities. Such examples illustrate the ongoing evolution of gender roles within faith traditions, highlighting the potential for growth and transformation as communities engage with modern challenges.

6.4 LGBTQ+ Perspectives: Faith and Identity

In the quiet moments of reflection, I often think about the complex relationship between faith and LGBTQ+ identities. Historically, many religious doctrines have positioned themselves in opposition to LGBTQ+ inclusion, citing specific passages as justification. Within Christianity, certain biblical verses have been interpreted to condemn homosexuality, creating a narrative that has long excluded LGBTQ+ individuals from full participation in the faith. Similarly, other major world religions have maintained traditional stances that often limit the acceptance of LGBTQ+ identities, reflecting broader cultural norms and historical contexts. These interpretations have shaped the experiences of countless individuals, leading to a fraught relationship between personal identity and spiritual belonging.

The experiences of LGBTQ+ individuals within religious contexts are as varied as they are profound. Many have faced exclusion, finding themselves marginalized within their communities and struggling to reconcile their identity with their faith. I recall conversations with friends who shared their stories of feeling unwelcome in the very places they once found solace. These narratives often include tales of rejection, where coming out led to estrangement from faith communities. Yet, amidst these challenges, there are also stories of acceptance and triumph. Some congregations have embraced LGBTQ+ members, offering a space where they can express their identity without fear. Personal narratives tell of individuals who have found ways to reconcile their faith with their identity, crafting a spiritual life that honors both. This reconciliation is a deeply personal journey that requires courage and introspection.

There's a growing shift within some religious groups towards greater LGBTQ+ inclusion. Progressive Christian denominations have begun reinterpreting doctrines to affirm LGBTQ+ rights, recognizing the need for a more inclusive approach to spirituality. These communities are reexamining traditional teachings, seeking to harmonize them with contemporary understandings of love and acceptance. Interfaith dialogues have also played a crucial role in this evolution, bringing together diverse voices to explore the intersection of faith and identity. These conversations foster empathy and understanding, encouraging religious institutions to consider the lived experiences of LGBTQ+ individuals. As these discussions unfold, they challenge long-held beliefs, paving the way for a more inclusive and compassionate faith.

LGBTQ+ faith activism is making significant strides in transforming religious institutions from within. LGBTQ+ clergy are leading inclusive congregations where acceptance is preached and practiced. These leaders advocate for change, working tirelessly to create communities that reflect the diversity of the human experience. Advocacy groups are also pushing for policy changes within religious organizations, aiming to dismantle structures that perpetuate exclusion. These efforts often involve working with religious leaders and engaging in dialogue to promote understanding and acceptance. Through workshops, educational programs, and public campaigns, these groups raise awareness and foster environments where every individual can thrive. Their work highlights the potential for faith communities to evolve, embracing the rich tapestry of human identity.

6.5 Technology and Spirituality: The Digital Faith Frontier

In recent years, technology has woven itself into the fabric of daily life, reshaping how we communicate and experience faith. The intersection of technology and spirituality presents new opportunities and challenges for religious communities. Virtual religious services have become a staple for many, especially during times when gathering in person is not feasible. These online worship platforms allow congregants to participate from the comfort of their homes, breaking down geographical barriers and creating a sense of unity across distances. Digital prayer tools and religious apps offer believers a way to integrate their faith practices into their daily routines, providing reminders for prayer times, scriptural readings, and even guided meditations. These technological advancements offer a sense of immediacy and accessibility, transforming how individuals engage with their spirituality.

Social media, too, plays a significant role in shaping modern faith communities. Platforms like Instagram, Twitter, and Facebook have become spaces where religious expression finds new forms. Online religious influencers share insights, reflections, and teachings with broad audiences, sparking conversations and creating virtual communities centered around shared beliefs. These influencers, often charismatic and relatable, have the power to inspire, challenge, and connect individuals who might never meet in person. Hashtags and movements promoting faith-based activism have gained momentum, drawing attention to social justice issues, environmental stewardship, and community support. These digital movements harness the power of collective action, allowing individuals to engage with and support causes that align with their spiritual values.

Technology's rapid advancement also poses challenges to traditional beliefs and practices. Ethical concerns arise with the use of artificial intelligence in religious decision-making, where the reliance on algorithms and data analytics can feel at odds with faith-based discernment. As technology alters religious rituals and practices, it raises questions about authenticity and the essence of spiritual experiences. For instance, can the use of virtual reality to simulate sacred sites provide a genuine sense of pilgrimage and connection? These are the questions that many faith communities grapple with, striving to balance innovation with tradition and the tangible with the virtual.

Some communities are embracing this digital transformation with creativity and openness. Churches, for example, have turned to live-streaming to reach remote congregants, ensuring that those unable to attend in person still feel connected to their spiritual community. These services often include interactive elements, such as live chats and digital offerings, fostering a sense of participation and engagement. Virtual reality experiences of sacred sites allow believers to explore places of spiritual significance from afar. These immersive experiences provide a new way to connect with the divine, offering a sense of presence and awe that transcends physical limitations. Through these innovative practices, technology becomes a tool that enhances rather than diminishes spiritual connection, bridging gaps and creating new pathways for expression.

As technology continues to evolve, it reshapes the landscape of spirituality, offering new possibilities for connection, expression, and growth.

6.6 Environmental Stewardship: Faith-Based Activism

In the quiet of a Sunday morning service, the preacher spoke of Genesis, reminding us that humanity was given dominion over the earth. This passage, like many others, has long been interpreted as a call to stewardship, urging believers to care for creation with responsibility and respect. Across various faiths, scriptural references highlight this duty. In Christianity, verses from the Bible advocate for the care of the earth, framing it as a divine mandate. Similarly, Islamic teachings emphasize harmony with nature, reminding believers of their role as earth stewards. The Quran speaks of the balance within creation, urging followers to maintain it. These doctrines call for a relationship with nature that is symbiotic and nurturing, recognizing the earth as a divine gift entrusted to humanity.

Amidst growing environmental concerns, faith-based environmental movements have emerged, driven by a desire to respond to ecological crises with action grounded in spiritual conviction. Interfaith coalitions are increasingly common, bringing together diverse religious communities united by a shared commitment to environmental preservation. These groups address climate change through advocacy, education, and community initiatives, emphasizing the moral imperative to protect the planet for future generations. Religious institutions, too, are adopting sustainable practices, integrating environmental stewardship into their daily operations. Churches, mosques, and temples are implementing energy-efficient technologies, encouraging recycling, and promoting sustainable agriculture. These efforts reflect a broader recognition of the interconnectedness between faith and the environment, illustrating a shift towards more ecologically responsible practices.

However, aligning environmental activism with religious doctrines is not without its challenges. Balancing economic needs with ecological responsibilities can create tension as communities grapple with the implications of sustainable practices on livelihoods and growth. For instance, transitioning to renewable energy sources may initially strain financial resources, posing a challenge for faith-based organizations striving to lead by example. Theological debates also arise over humanity's role in environmental conservation. Some argue for a more interventionist approach, seeking to manage and control natural resources, while others advocate for allowing natural processes to unfold with minimal human interference. These discussions highlight the complexities of integrating faith with environmentalism, requiring nuanced consideration of ethical, theological, and practical concerns.

Despite these challenges, numerous faith-based initiatives have demonstrated the potential for religious communities to lead effective environmental efforts. Take, for example, a Buddhist temple in Thailand that has implemented zero-waste policies. By embracing principles of mindfulness and simplicity, the temple encourages its community to reduce waste, compost organic materials, and recycle diligently. These practices not only reduce the temple's environmental footprint but also serve as a model for the surrounding community, inspiring broader change. In another instance, Christian congregations across the United States have organized community clean-up projects, mobilizing members to restore local parks, waterways, and neighborhoods. These efforts foster a sense of collective responsibility, reinforcing the connection between faith and action.

As we consider the role of faith in environmental stewardship, it becomes clear that religious communities possess unique resources and perspectives that can drive meaningful change. By drawing on spiritual teachings and communal values, faith-based organizations have the potential to lead the way in addressing environmental challenges. Their efforts reflect a growing awareness of the moral and ethical dimensions of environmentalism, highlighting the power of faith to inspire action and transformation.

CHAPTER 7

OVERCOMING FEAR AND JUDGMENT

On a sunny afternoon at a bustling coffee shop, I overheard a conversation that resonated deeply. A young woman, seated across from her friend, recounted her struggles with criticism from her religious community. Her voice, though steady, carried the weight of judgment she felt for questioning traditional beliefs. This moment, a snapshot of vulnerability and resilience, encapsulated the complex dance between fear and judgment many of us encounter on our spiritual paths. It reminded me of the times I, too, faced external criticism, both from within religious circles and from secular skeptics who viewed faith as an irrational endeavor.

Across the spectrum of faith communities, judgment often arises from the expectation to adhere to established doctrines. The pressure to conform can be overwhelming, especially when your beliefs begin to diverge from the norm. From whispered remarks at gatherings to direct confrontations, the message is clear: deviation is not always welcome. This pressure is compounded by secular criticisms, where faith can be dismissed as naive or unscientific. In a world that increasingly values empirical evidence and logic, spirituality can sometimes be seen as anachronistic, leading to further alienation.

Responding to such criticism with grace requires a balance of understanding and resilience. It begins with practicing active listening, a skill that involves hearing the critic's perspective without immediately crafting a defense. By genuinely engaging with their viewpoint, you can uncover underlying concerns or misconceptions that may be addressed through open dialogue. Responding with empathy and acknowledging their emotions without necessarily agreeing can diffuse tension and foster mutual understanding. However, it's crucial to recognize when a conversation ceases to be productive. Setting boundaries and knowing when to disengage from negative dialogues protect your emotional well-being and maintain your integrity.

Building resilience is vital to weathering external judgment. Developing a metaphorical thick skin can help desensitize you to unconstructive criticism, allowing you to focus on what truly matters. This doesn't mean becoming indifferent but discerning which critiques merit consideration and which do not. Emphasizing your inner values and strengthening your self-worth independent of external opinions fortifies your sense of self. This inner strength becomes a sanctuary, a reminder that your worth is not determined by others' perceptions but by your determined convictions.

Consider the story of an activist who, amidst public scrutiny, maintained composure and grace. Her advocacy, though controversial, was anchored in deeply held beliefs about justice and equality. Despite harsh criticism, she listened actively, engaging with dissenting voices to understand their perspectives. Through empathy, she built bridges where walls once stood, demonstrating that resilience and openness could transform opposition into dialogue. Similarly, a spiritual leader faced criticism head-on by acknowledging concerns with transparency and understanding. By doing so, he fostered a community grounded in trust, where differing viewpoints could coexist harmoniously.

Reflection Section: Navigating External Judgment

- Identify Criticism Sources: Reflect on where external judgment in your life comes from. Is it from religious peers, secular circles, or both?

- Practice Active Listening: Listen without preparing a defense next time you face criticism. What can you learn from the critic's perspective?

- Set Boundaries: Know when to disengage from unproductive dialogues. Consider how setting boundaries can protect your peace and integrity.

Through these reflections, you can find ways to navigate criticism with grace and resilience, transforming potential conflict into opportunities for growth. As you continue this journey, remember that external judgments, while challenging, are not definitive. They are merely reflections of others' perceptions and do not define your spiritual path.

7.1 Inner Critic: Overcoming Self-Doubt and Fear

One afternoon, as I sat with my thoughts, I felt the familiar presence of my inner critic. This voice, often uninvited, seemed to magnify every flaw and mistake, casting a shadow over my achievements. It's a voice many of us know well, born from internalized beliefs and fears, whispering doubts that erode our confidence. Perfectionism, with its impossible standards, fuels this critic. It demands flawlessness and leaves no room for error, creating relentless pressure to meet unrealistic expectations. Alongside it, the fear of failure looms large. The anxiety of making mistakes in our spiritual or personal growth can be paralyzing, stalling progress and keeping us from pursuing our true potential.

The inner critic's impact on self-esteem is profound. Negative self-talk can become a cycle, where each critical thought feeds the next, creating a loop of doubt and insecurity. It's like a storm that gathers strength with every gust, turning minor to silence the inner critic missteps into perceived catastrophes. Imposter syndrome often accompanies this cycle, making us feel like frauds despite our accomplishments. We question our worthiness of success, whether in our careers, relationships, or spiritual endeavors, convinced that we are not as capable as others perceive. This persistent self-doubt can undermine confidence, leaving us feeling unworthy of the achievements we'vWesilence the inner critic, we must first transform our negative self-talk into positive affirmation. Cognitive restructuring is a powerful tool for this transformation. We can shift our perspective by consciously reframing negative thoughts into constructive narratives. For example, instead of dwelling on a perceived failure, we might recognize it as a valuable learning experience. Affirmation practices also play a crucial role in reinforcing self-worth. Daily positive affirmations remind us of our strengths and capabilities, slowly replacing the critic's voice with one of encouragement and support. Mindfulness meditation further aids this process by allowing us to observe and release self-critical thoughts without judgment. Through mindfulness, we learn to acknowledge these thoughts without letting them define us, creating space for self-compassion and growth.

Consider the story of a writer who, plagued by fear, hesitated to publish her personal spiritual journey. Her inner critic insisted that her words were inadequate and that her story lacked significance. Yet, through affirmations and cognitive restructuring, she began to view her work with fresh eyes. She realized that her journey, though personal, held the potential to resonate with others. Embracing self-compassion, she silenced her critic and shared her story, finding both success and fulfillment in the process. Similarly, an individual struggling with perfectionism found freedom by embracing self-compassion. He learned to appreciate his efforts and progress by acknowledging that perfection is unattainable. This shift allowed him to break free from the critic's grip, finding joy in his accomplishments without the constant burden of perfection.

These narratives illustrate the power of confronting and overcoming the inner critic. By transforming negative self-talk, practicing mindfulness, and embracing self-compassion, we can break the cycle of self-doubt. This journey requires patience and persistence, but we reclaim our confidence and sense of self-worth with each step. The critic's voice, once so loud and persistent, begins to fade, replaced by a kinder, more supportive inner dialogue. Through these practices, we learn to trust ourselves and our abilities, allowing us to move forward with confidence and courage.

7.2 Finding Strength in Vulnerability: Embracing Authenticity

Sitting alone in a park, surrounded by the quiet rustle of leaves, I realized that vulnerability was not the weakness I once believed it to be. It is, in fact, a profound strength. It requires courage to open oneself to the world and reveal the truths beneath the surface. In spiritual growth, vulnerability becomes a powerful tool. It allows for deeper connections with others, fostering relationships built on authenticity and trust. By embracing vulnerability, we let go of facades and embrace who we truly are, unburdened by the expectations of others. This openness, this raw honesty, becomes a wellspring of resilience, fortifying us against life's challenges.

Yet, the path to vulnerability is fraught with challenges. The fear of rejection looms large, a shadow that whispers of misunderstandings and judgment. To be vulnerable is to expose the very parts we often guard most fiercely, risking emotional exposure. Navigating this discomfort requires bravery, as it means facing the possibility that everyone might not embrace our true selves. This fear can be paralyzing, keeping us locked in a cycle of self-preservation that stifles growth and prevents genuine connection. The risk of being open, of laying bare one's soul, is daunting, and it is only natural to shy away from such exposure. But by confronting these fears, we unlock the potential for profound transformation.

To cultivate vulnerability, one must begin by practicing self-disclosure. Sharing personal stories, revealing the experiences that have shaped us, builds bridges between hearts. It is through these narratives that we connect, finding common ground in shared struggles and triumphs. By speaking our truths, we invite others to do the same, creating a space where authenticity flourishes. Building a supportive network is also crucial. Finding trusted individuals with whom to share vulnerabilities provides a safety net, a circle of understanding and compassion. These connections become vital, offering support and encouragement as we navigate the complexities of openness.

Consider the story of a community leader who, through the lens of personal struggles, inspired and connected with those around her. By embracing her vulnerabilities, she fostered a sense of unity, demonstrating that strength lies not in perfection but in the willingness to be imperfectly human. Her openness resonated, encouraging others to share their own stories and creating a community grounded in empathy and support. Or think of a spiritual seeker who found deeper meaning through authentic expression. By allowing himself to be vulnerable, to question and explore without fear of judgment, he uncovered layers of his spirituality that had long been hidden. Through this process, he discovered a profound connection to himself and those around him, illustrating the transformative power of authenticity.

Embracing vulnerability is not a singular act but an ongoing commitment to live authentically. It is the choice to show up, to be seen, and to engage fully with the world. This journey toward authenticity is both challenging and rewarding, inviting us to step into the fullness of who we are, unencumbered by the masks we often wear. We find strength, connection, and a deeper understanding of our place within the world through vulnerability.

7.3 Transforming Fear into Courage: The Path to Empowerment

Fear is a formidable presence in our lives, often lurking in the shadows of the unknown. It whispers doubts about the future, weaving anxiety about uncertainties in faith and life. This fear of the unknown can paralyze you, leaving you hesitant to explore new spiritual territories or make decisions that could lead to growth. It's a visceral reaction to the unpredictability of life, where every path seems fraught with potential pitfalls. Similarly, the fear of change acts as a formidable barrier, anchoring you to comfort zones that feel safe but ultimately hinder progress. Change challenges the familiar, asking you to step into the unknown with no guarantee of success. The resistance to leaving these zones, where routines are predictable and secure, can be so intense that it stifles potential, keeping you from realizing your true capabilities.

Yet, within these fears lies the seed of courage. Transforming fear into courage begins with a choice, a conscious decision to face fears head-on. Courage isn't the absence of fear; it's the resolve to act despite it. By acknowledging fear as a natural response, you can reframe it as an opportunity for growth and empowerment. This shift in mindset is pivotal. It requires seeing fear not as a barrier but as a catalyst for action, a push towards confronting what holds you back. This perspective turns fear into a powerful motivator rather than an insurmountable obstacle, inviting you to embrace challenges with determination.

Cultivating courage involves practical strategies that build confidence and resilience. Visualization techniques can be particularly effective, allowing you to imagine successful outcomes and foster belief in your abilities. By picturing yourself overcoming obstacles, you create a mental blueprint for success, reinforcing the possibility of achievement. Incremental challenges are another valuable tool. By gradually facing fears, you build resilience, strengthening your ability to confront more significant challenges over time. This step-by-step approach makes daunting tasks more manageable, breaking them into achievable parts. Support systems, too, play a crucial role. Leaning on community and mentors offers encouragement and guidance, providing a network of strength to draw upon when fear threatens to overwhelm them. These networks act as pillars, offering reassurance and perspective when doubts arise.

Consider the story of a woman who, once paralyzed by the fear of public speaking, found her voice through advocacy. Initially, the thought of addressing an audience filled her with dread, the spotlight a glaring reminder of her insecurities. However, she confronted this fear, visualizing herself speaking confidently and gracefully. Gradually, she took small steps, speaking in front of supportive friends and mentors who cheered her on. Each success built upon the last until she stood before larger audiences, her voice a powerful instrument for social change. Her courage not only overcame fear but transformed it into a tool for empowerment, enabling her to champion causes she believed in deeply.

Another individual found empowerment by embracing change and pursuing a new spiritual path despite initial trepidation. The comfort of familiar beliefs was a safety net he hesitated to cut away. Yet, drawn by a longing for deeper understanding, he explored different spiritual practices. This decision required courage, as it meant leaving behind the certainty of what he knew. Through visualization and incremental steps, he ventured into new spiritual communities, each encounter enriching his understanding and strengthening his resolve. Support from mentors who had walked similar paths bolstered his courage, enabling him to confidently navigate this new terrain.

These stories illustrate how fear, when confronted with courage, can be transformed into a source of empowerment. By embracing fear as a stepping stone rather than a stumbling block, you can unlock potential and discover strengths you never knew existed. Courage becomes not just a response to fear but a way of life, guiding you toward a more empowered and authentic self.

CHAPTER 8

INSPIRATIONAL AND MOTIVATIONAL CONTENT

There is a unique stillness just after a storm, a moment when the world feels both fragile and powerful. This is how I felt one evening, sitting with a friend who had just weathered a personal tempest. Her story was one of profound loss and undeniable strength, weaving a tale of resilience that mirrored the broader themes of our shared human experience. In her eyes, I saw both the weight of her past struggles and the light of her newfound liberation. This chapter is dedicated to stories like hers—narratives of individuals who have faced significant spiritual crises and emerged with renewed faith and purpose. These stories are not just about overcoming adversity; they are about transformation and the enduring power of the human spirit.

One such tale is that of a woman who found herself navigating the choppy waters of grief after losing her partner. Her faith, once a beacon of hope, now felt distant and unreachable. In the weeks that followed, she grappled with questions that seemed to have no answers. It was during a spiritual retreat, nestled in the quiet embrace of nature that she began to find her footing again. Surrounded by the whispers of the wind and the gentle rustling of leaves, she felt a profound sense of connection to something greater than herself. This retreat marked a turning point, a moment of clarity where she reconciled her faith with her loss. It was here that she discovered the strength that lay within her, the resilience that had been quietly growing amidst the chaos.

Another story that resonates deeply is that of an ex-clergy member who left behind the ministry he had dedicated his life to. Disillusioned and adrift, he questioned the very essence of his calling. It was a community of fellow seekers, each on their own path of discovery, that provided the solace and support he so desperately needed. Through their shared stories and collective wisdom, he began to see his journey not as a failure but as a new beginning. This community became his sanctuary, a place where he could rebuild his spiritual identity without the constraints of dogma. Here, he found a deeply personal and liberating renewed sense of purpose.

These turning points, whether found in the solitude of a retreat or the embrace of a community, are often the catalysts for profound personal breakthroughs. They serve as reminders that the path to healing is not linear but a series of moments that guide us toward renewal. Such experiences often lead to significant emotional and spiritual changes. The woman who reconciled her faith after loss grew in empathy, her understanding of others deepened by her own journey through the shadows. Similarly, the ex-clergy member developed a more nuanced belief system that celebrated the diversity of spiritual expression and embraced the beauty of uncertainty.

From these narratives, several lessons emerge, offering insights that can be applied to your own life. Perseverance in the face of doubt is crucial. It's about holding onto hope when the path is shrouded in darkness, trusting that light will find its way through. Embracing uncertainty as a catalyst for growth allows you to find strength in vulnerability, transforming fear into a source of empowerment. These stories teach us that faith is not about having all the answers but about being open to the questions leading to your brealthrough and finding solace in the journey and the wisdom it brings.

Reflection Exercise: Finding Your Turning Point

- Identify a Personal Challenge: Reflect on a time when you faced a significant spiritual or personal challenge. What emotions did you experience, and how did they impact your beliefs?

- Recognize Your Turning Point: Consider the key moments or realizations that led to your personal breakthrough. Was there a specific event, person, or experience that helped you find clarity?

- Apply the Lessons: Think about the lessons you learned from this experience. How can they guide you in your current journey, and how might they help you navigate future challenges?

Remember, each story is a testament to the resilience of the human spirit, offering hope and inspiration as you continue to explore and embrace your own path.

8.1 Inspirational Figures: Learning from Spiritual Guides

In the tapestry of human history, certain figures stand out, not just for their accomplishments, but for the profound spiritual impact they have made. Mahatma Gandhi and Mother Teresa are two such luminaries whose lives continue to inspire and guide countless individuals around the globe. Gandhi wove these principles into the fabric of India's struggle for independence with his unyielding commitment to non-violence and truth. His philosophy of Satyagraha, or "truth force," was not just a political strategy but a spiritual discipline. Gandhi believed that real change must begin with the individual and that non-violence was a powerful weapon against injustice. His integration of spirituality and activism created a movement that not only liberated a nation but also inspired global peace initiatives, reminding us that true strength lies in compassion and understanding.

Mother Teresa, on the other hand, dedicated her life to serving those society often overlooks. Her work with the poorest of the poor in Calcutta exemplified a profound commitment to love and compassion. Mother Teresa's philosophy was simple yet profound: every act of kindness is an act of love towards God. She taught that serving the marginalized is not just charity but a humble recognition of our shared humanity. Her tireless efforts earned her the Nobel Peace Prize and inspired a worldwide movement of service and compassion. Through her actions, she demonstrated that small acts of kindness could weave together to create a tapestry of immense beauty and hope.

The impact of Gandhi's and Mother Teresa's work extends far beyond their immediate context. Gandhi's teachings have been a beacon for peace movements worldwide, influencing leaders such as Martin Luther King Jr. and Nelson Mandela. His philosophy of non-violence challenges us to look beyond anger and vengeance to seek justice through peace and reconciliation. It invites individuals to apply these principles in their own lives, fostering environments of understanding and mutual respect. Mother Teresa's legacy, too, lives on in the countless lives she touched. Her example inspires people to embrace the power of service, to see the divine in every human being, and to respond with compassion and love. Personal stories abound of those who have found transformation through her teachings, whether by volunteering in their communities or simply offering a smile to a stranger.

From these influential figures, there are practical lessons we can incorporate into our lives. Practicing non-violent communication, inspired by Gandhi, encourages us to express ourselves honestly and empathetically, fostering healthier relationships. It teaches us to listen actively, to seek understanding rather than conflict, and to respond with compassion even in the face of disagreement. This approach can transform interactions, creating spaces where dialogue replaces discord. Engaging in acts of service, following Mother

Teresa's example, allows us to cultivate compassion and humility. Whether volunteering at a local shelter or helping a neighbor, these acts remind us of our interconnectedness and the profound impact of small gestures.

These lessons are not just philosophical musings; they are calls to action. They challenge us to live with integrity, to align our actions with our beliefs, and to make a tangible difference in the world around us. As you reflect on the lives of Gandhi and Mother Teresa, consider how their teachings might inform your own spiritual practice. How might you incorporate non-violence and service into your daily life? What small changes can you make to foster a more compassionate and understanding world? These figures remind us that even in the darkest moments, there is always a path illuminated by love, truth, and compassion.

8.2 Motivational Messages: Finding Hope Amidst Doubt

In moments of uncertainty, when doubt seems to overshadow everything, holding onto simple yet profound truths can illuminate the path ahead. Consider the phrase "This too shall pass." It's more than just a saying; it's a reminder of life's ever-changing nature, offering comfort and perspective. Challenges, no matter how overwhelming, are temporary. They ebb and flow like the tides, and recognizing their fleeting nature can bring solace. Similarly, "Every doubt is a doorway to deeper understanding" encourages you to view uncertainty not as a barrier but as an invitation to explore. Doubt prompts questions, and questions lead to insight and growth. Embracing this mindset can transform fear into curiosity, fostering resilience and strength.

Affirmations are powerful tools that can shift your mindset and nurture resilience. By repeating positive statements, you can rewire your thought patterns, creating new pathways in the brain that support confidence and hope. Crafting personal affirmations involves focusing on what you wish to embody. It might be as simple as saying, "I am capable of navigating life's challenges," or "I trust the journey I am on." These statements, when spoken regularly, become anchors in times of turmoil. There are countless stories of individuals who have overcome doubt through the use of affirmations. One example is a young woman who, after experiencing a series of setbacks, began each day by affirming her worth and potential. Over time, these words became her truth, guiding her toward new opportunities and a renewed sense of purpose.

Gratitude, too, plays a vital role in maintaining hope. By focusing on what you have rather than what you lack, gratitude can transform your perspective, lifting you from despair to appreciation Keeping a gratitude journal is a simple yet effective practice. Each day, jot down a few things you're thankful for, whether it's a kind gesture from a friend, the beauty of a sunset, or the comfort of a warm home. This practice shifts your focus to the positive and enhances your emotional well-being and resilience. Studies have shown that those who regularly practice gratitude experience greater happiness and lower stress levels. It's a reminder that even in difficult times, there are always moments of light to hold onto.

In cultivating hope, practical exercises can reinforce positivity and resilience. Visualization exercises can be particularly effective when you imagine positive outcomes and the steps to achieve them. Picture yourself overcoming obstacles, feeling the emotions of success and relief. This practice not only boosts confidence but also prepares your mind to tackle challenges with clarity and determination. Mindfulness practices focusing on present-moment awareness further enhance this process. By grounding yourself in the now, you reduce anxiety and create space for calm and clarity. Simple mindfulness exercises, like focused breathing or mindful walking, help center your thoughts and bring peace amidst the chaos.

Incorporating these practices into your daily life can create a sanctuary within, a place of peace and strength. As you navigate the complexities of faith and doubt, remember that hope is not a distant destination but a state of being that you can cultivate each day. Through affirmations, gratitude, visualization, and mindfulnessYou can nurture this hope through, allowing it to guide you through even the darkest times. These tools are your companions, reminding you of the light within and the possibilities that lie ahead.

8.3 Embracing the Journey: Finding Joy in Exploration

Imagine standing on the shore, gazing out at the endless ocean, each wave a mystery waiting to be discovered. This is the essence of spiritual exploration—an ever-unfolding journey where the beauty lies not in the destination but in the questions that guide us. Unanswered questions hold a particular allure, sparking curiosity and inviting you to seek deeper truths. It's in the space between knowing and not knowing that growth occurs. Embracing this uncertainty can transform your spiritual path into an exciting adventure. Each insight, no matter how small, becomes a victory, a stepping stone on the path to understanding. Celebrating these moments fosters a spirit of gratitude and wonder, reminding you that even in the smallest discoveries, there is profound beauty.

To fully embrace this exploration, maintain a curious and open mindset. Curiosity fuels your desire to learn, pushing you to engage with diverse spiritual practices and traditions. Whether attending a meditation session inspired by Eastern philosophies or participating in a community ritual from a different culture, each experience broadens your understanding. Through this engagement, empathy deepens, allowing you to connect with others on a more meaningful level. Curiosity, when nurtured, becomes a tool for breaking down barriers and fostering a sense of unity amidst diversity. It encourages you to step outside your comfort zone and view the world through new lenses, enriching your spiritual tapestry with a myriad of colors and textures.

The joy found in spiritual exploration is often reflected in the stories of those who have embraced this path. Take the traveler who, while journeying through distant lands, discovered profound insights through cultural exchanges. Each encounter, whether with a local artisan or a fellow wanderer, became a lesson in humility and interconnectedness. These experiences highlighted the shared human spirit, transcending borders and beliefs. Or consider the artist who channels spirituality through creative endeavors. For them, each brushstroke or note is an expression of the divine, a tangible representation of the intangible. Through their art, they find solace and meaning, creating a dialogue between the seen and unseen. These narratives illuminate how joy can manifest in exploration, each unique yet universally resonant.

Consider integrating practical strategies into your daily life to cultivate joy in your spiritual exploration. Setting intentions for your spiritual practices can provide direction and purpose. Begin each day with a simple intention, such as seeking peace or fostering compassion. This practice aligns your actions with your values, creating a harmonious flow throughout your day. Balancing goal-setting with appreciation for the present moment ensures you remain grounded in the here and now. It's easy to become consumed by future aspirations, but true joy lies in savoring each moment. Whether through mindfulness exercises, like deep breathing or gratitude journaling, these practices help anchor you in the present, allowing you to experience the richness of each day fully.

These practices, stories, and perspectives remind you that spiritual exploration is a lifelong pursuit filled with endless opportunities for growth and discovery. By embracing curiosity, celebrating small victories, and engaging with diverse traditions, you cultivate a sense of joy and fulfillment on your path. As you continue to explore, remember that the journey itself is the destination, and every step taken with an open heart is a step toward further understanding and connection.

CHAPTER 9

PRACTICAL SOLUTIONS FOR FAITH INTEGRATION

Imagine waking up to the first whispers of dawn, your room gently lit by the soft glow of a single candle. The world outside is still, offering a rare moment of peace before the demands of the day unfold. You pause, inhaling deeply, as you light the candle with intention, its flickering flame a beacon of hope and clarity. This simple act is not just about lighting a wick; it's a ritual, a daily practice that sets the foundation for the day ahead. In our often chaotic lives, establishing consistent spiritual practices can serve as anchors, grounding us amidst the stormy seas of doubt and uncertainty.

The concept of daily spiritual practices might sound daunting, but it's about integrating small, meaningful rituals into your day. These practices are not about grand gestures but the accumulation of small acts that reinforce faith consistently. Starting your day with a moment of meditation or prayer can center your thoughts, aligning them with your values and intentions. Imagine beginning each morning with a few minutes of stillness, allowing your mind to settle and your spirit to awaken. This practice invites a sense of calm and focus, preparing you to face the day with a centered heart.

Evening reflections offer another touchpoint, a time to journal your gratitude or lessons learned, providing closure to the day's events. As the sun sets, take a moment to reflect on the day's experiences. What brought you joy? What challenged you? By capturing these thoughts in a journal, you create a space for gratitude and growth. This ritual helps you recognize the small blessings often overlooked in the rush of daily life. It's a gentle reminder of the beauty that exists even in mundane moments, fostering a sense of appreciation and awareness.

Consistent spiritual rituals offer numerous benefits, grounding you in routine and enhancing mindfulness. They provide a framework for stability, a touchstone in the ever-shifting landscape of life. By establishing a routine, you build a sense of security and peace, creating a sanctuary amidst chaos. These rituals enhance mindfulness, encouraging you to stay present through repetitive actions. Each small act, whether lighting a candle or jotting down a gratitude list, serves as a reminder to pause and appreciate the present moment.

Consider incorporating simple daily rituals that resonate with your personal beliefs and lifestyle. Lighting a candle with a morning intention can be a powerful start to the day, its flame symbolizing hope and clarity. Taking mindful walks in nature offers a chance to connect with the divine, grounding yourself in the beauty of the natural world. Practicing a daily mantra for focus and clarity can help center your thoughts, aligning them with your spiritual goals. These practices are not about perfection but about finding what works for you and adapting them to fit your unique journey.

Reflection Exercise: Crafting Your Rituals

1. Morning Intention: Choose a simple act like lighting a candle to start your day. Reflect on a word or theme you wish to embody, such as "peace" or "courage."

2. Evening Reflection: Set aside time each night to jot down three things you are grateful for. Consider how these moments brought beauty or insight into your day.

3. Nature Connection: Incorporate a short walk into your day, focusing on the sights, sounds, and sensations around you. Allow this practice to connect you with the world outside.

These simple rituals have the power to transform your spiritual life. A busy professional once shared how a five-minute morning meditation brought peace amidst the chaos of corporate life. Similarly, a parent found that integrating spiritual lessons into family meals enriched their relationships and deepened their practice. By weaving these practices into your daily routine, you create a tapestry of faith and mindfulness that supports and nurtures your spiritual journey.

9.1 Faith in Action: Living Beliefs Through Service

Imagine walking into a bustling community center on a crisp Saturday morning, the air buzzing with energy as volunteers gather to prepare meals for those in need. The smell of freshly baked bread fills the room, mingling with the sound of laughter and conversation. This is more than just an act of kindness; it's an expression of faith in action. When we engage in service, we breathe life into our beliefs, transforming them from abstract concepts into tangible acts of love and compassion. Volunteering for local charities allows us to directly impact our communities, fostering a sense of shared responsibility and collective growth. By organizing faith-driven initiatives, we can create projects that reflect our spiritual values, addressing issues that resonate deeply with our hearts.

Service is a powerful catalyst for spiritual growth, offering opportunities to deepen our faith and discover a sense of purpose. Through serving others, we build empathy and compassion, gaining a deeper understanding of the diverse life experiences that shape our world. As we interact with individuals from various backgrounds, we recognize the interconnectedness of the human condition, realizing that beneath our differences lies a shared humanity. This realization fosters humility and gratitude, reminding us of the blessings in our own lives and inspiring us to give back. Service also provides a sense of fulfillment as we witness the positive impact of our actions on those we serve. It reminds us that we are part of something larger than ourselves, a community bound by a common desire to uplift and support one another.

There are countless ways to engage in service that align with your faith and values. Participating in environmental clean-up efforts is a meaningful way to care for the earth, honoring the divine creation that sustains us. Imagine spending a day by a riverbank, removing debris and restoring the natural beauty of the landscape. This act not only benefits the environment but also nurtures a connection to the natural world, reminding us of our role as stewards of the planet. Mentoring youth through faith-based programs offers another avenue for service, providing guidance and support to the next generation. By sharing your experiences and wisdom, you can inspire young minds, helping them navigate the challenges of adolescence with confidence and resilience. Assisting at food banks or shelters is yet another way to make a difference, addressing the immediate needs of those facing hardship. These opportunities allow you to extend compassion and kindness, offering a helping hand to those in need.

Consider the story of a community leader who found personal fulfillment through activism. Driven by a passion for social justice, she organized a grassroots campaign to address food insecurity in her neighborhood. Her efforts brought together volunteers, local businesses, and government agencies, creating a network of support that transformed the lives of countless families. Through her work, she discovered a new spiritual calling, one that aligned her personal beliefs with her desire to serve others. Similarly, an individual volunteering at a local shelter found a profound sense of purpose in helping those experiencing homelessness. The relationships he built with the shelter residents opened his eyes to the resilience and strength of the human spirit, inspiring him to pursue a career in social work.

These stories illustrate the transformative power of service, showing how living our beliefs through action can lead to profound spiritual growth. By engaging in service, we not only strengthen our faith but also contribute to the well-being of our communities, building a world rooted in love, compassion, and understanding. As we continue to explore the ways in which faith can guide and enrich our lives, let us remember the impact of our actions, embracing the call to serve with open hearts and willing hands.

9.2 Navigating Faith in Relationships: Building Supportive Bonds

Faith often finds its deepest expression not in solitude but in the relationships we nurture. When shared beliefs align, they can serve as a powerful bond, weaving together the fabric of connection and understanding. These shared spiritual foundations provide a common language and a shared vision that strengthens emotional ties and fosters deeper intimacy. However, navigating the complexities of faith in relationships requires sensitivity, particularly when beliefs diverge. It's crucial to communicate your faith with partners in a way that invites dialogue and understanding rather than imposition. This approach respects the autonomy of each individual, allowing space for both shared and diverse spiritual paths to coexist harmoniously.

In families and friendships, respecting diverse spiritual paths is paramount. This involves honoring the differences that may arise, recognizing that each person's journey is unique. When family members or friends hold different beliefs, it's an opportunity to learn and grow, to see the world through another's eyes. This respect doesn't mean you must agree with their beliefs, but it involves acknowledging their right to hold them. It means engaging in open and respectful conversations, where listening becomes as essential as speaking. By doing so, you cultivate an environment of mutual respect and understanding, laying the groundwork for meaningful connections that transcend differences.

To integrate faith into relationships effectively, setting shared spiritual goals can be transformative. Whether deciding to meditate together once a week or volunteering for a cause you both care about, these shared goals create a unified vision for the future. They serve as a reminder of your common values and aspirations, anchoring your relationship in something greater than yourselves. Active listening is also key; it encourages open and respectful dialogue, allowing both parties to feel heard and valued. Through such exchanges, misunderstandings can be clarified, and empathy can flourish. Celebrating spiritual milestones together—such as anniversaries, religious holidays, or personal achievements— reinforces the bonds of shared experience and creates cherished memories.

Faith-centered relationships offer profound benefits, enhancing relational intimacy and understanding. Sharing spiritual practices, such as prayer or meditation, builds trust through shared values, strengthening emotional connections. These practices create a sacred space where partners can be vulnerable and authentic, fostering a deeper sense of belonging and security. As you grow together spiritually, you experience mutual growth, learning from each other's insights and perspectives. This shared journey enriches your relationship, making it a source of strength and inspiration. The process of learning and evolving together deepens your connection, cultivating a shared narrative that weaves your individual stories into a cohesive whole.

Consider the story of a couple who found harmony through interfaith dialogue. Despite coming from different religious backgrounds, they embraced their differences as opportunities for exploration and growth. Through open conversations and shared rituals, they created a unique spiritual practice that honored both traditions. Their relationship thrived, not despite their differences, but because of them. Similarly, a friendship deepened by shared meditation practices illustrates how spiritual alignment can enhance personal bonds. These friends found solace and support in their shared practice, using meditation as a means to connect and grow together. These examples highlight the potential for relationships to flourish when faith is integrated with respect and understanding.

Navigating faith in relationships is both an art and a practice. It involves balancing shared beliefs with individual paths, creating a tapestry of connection that is both diverse and unified. By engaging in open dialogue, setting shared goals, and respecting differences, you can build supportive bonds that enrich your spiritual journey. These relationships become a source of joy and fulfillment, offering a place where your faith can be expressed and celebrated.

9.3 Balancing Faith with Career: Maintaining Spiritual Integrity

In the bustling corridors of professional life, where deadlines loom, and responsibilities pile up, maintaining spiritual integrity can feel like a balancing act. With its numerous demands, the workplace often presents challenges that can test your values and beliefs. Navigating ethical dilemmas becomes a daily task as you strive to align professional decisions with personal convictions. This alignment is crucial, as it ensures that your actions reflect the core of who you are. Whether it's a decision about honesty in reporting or choosing sustainable practices over profit, these moments define your character and the legacy you leave behind.

Time, too, becomes a precious commodity. In the rush of meetings and commitments, finding moments for spiritual reflection can seem impossible. Yet, it is precisely in these hectic schedules that such moments are most needed. Managing time effectively to include spiritual practices requires intention and creativity. It might mean carving out a few minutes during your lunch break for a short meditation, a practice that can rejuvenate your spirit and clear your mind. These brief pauses are not mere luxuries; they are necessities that help maintain balance and perspective.

To uphold spiritual integrity at work, you might consider integrating personal rituals into your daily routine. These rituals, though simple, serve as constant reminders of your values. A short meditative break at your desk, where you close your eyes and focus on your breath, can provide a much-needed reset. Setting boundaries to honor your spiritual commitments is equally important. This might mean leaving work at a reasonable hour to attend a religious service or setting aside time for personal reflection at the end of the day. In doing so, you affirm that your spiritual well-being is as vital as your professional success.

Finding opportunities for faith-driven leadership can further strengthen your commitment to spiritual integrity. This involves leading by example, making decisions that reflect your beliefs, and inspiring others through your actions. It's about creating a work environment that values ethics and compassion, where colleagues feel respected and valued. Leadership rooted in faith is not about imposing beliefs but about embodying principles that uplift and inspire. It's about being a beacon of integrity that others can look up to, fostering a culture of mutual respect and understanding.

Aligning your career with your spiritual values offers profound benefits. It leads to greater job satisfaction and personal fulfillment as you find harmony between your work and your faith. Experiencing alignment means being true to yourself in all aspects of life, allowing your actions to flow naturally from your beliefs. This authenticity not only enriches your own experience but also inspires those around you. Through faith-based actions and decisions, you become a role model, showing how integrity and success can coexist. It demonstrates that living according to your values can lead to both professional achievement and personal happiness.

Consider the story of an entrepreneur who incorporated ethical principles into her business practices. By prioritizing transparency and sustainability, she not only built a successful company but also created a workplace culture that valued honesty and responsibility. Her commitment to these principles inspired her employees and attracted clients who shared similar values. In another example, a healthcare professional prioritized compassion and empathy in patient care. By treating each patient with dignity and kindness, she found deep satisfaction in her work and earned the trust and respect of her colleagues. Her approach transformed the patient experience, making care more holistic and humane.

These examples illustrate how spiritual integrity can be maintained and celebrated within the professional sphere. They show that it is possible to succeed without compromising your values and that faith can be a source of strength and guidance in the most challenging environments. As you navigate your career, remember that your faith is not a separate entity but an integral part of who you are. It is a guiding light that can illuminate your path, offering wisdom and clarity as you strive to live authentically and meaningfully.

CHAPTER 10

THE FUTURE OF FAITH AND DOUBT

In a sunlit library, I once found myself lost in the pages of a book on ancient philosophies. The room was filled with the scent of old paper and quiet wisdom, a sanctuary for the curious mind. It was here that I realized how much our beliefs are like those very books—constantly being rewritten with each new chapter of our lives. As we grow, our perspectives shift, influenced by the experiences and understandings that unfold with time. These shifts are part of the natural evolution of faith, reflecting the journey of discovery that is life itself.

Our beliefs are as dynamic as we are. They transform as we transition through different stages of life, maturing and expanding with age and experience. In youth, faith may be shaped by familial and cultural influences, absorbing the values and traditions handed down through generations. As we mature, these beliefs are challenged by the complexities of adulthood, prompting reevaluation and adaptation. The wisdom of age brings deeper reflection, often leading to a more nuanced understanding of spirituality. This evolution mirrors the cycles of life, where each phase offers new insights and opportunities for growth.

Cultural shifts also play a significant role in shaping our beliefs. As society evolves, so do the collective values and norms that influence faith. Historical trends reveal patterns of change within religious traditions and spiritual movements, highlighting the fluid nature of belief systems. The 19th and 20th centuries, for instance, witnessed the emergence of new religious movements, each responding to the social and political landscapes of their time. These movements reflect the dynamic interplay between faith and the broader cultural context, illustrating how beliefs adapt to meet the needs of the era. The Reformation is another example, a period of renewal that redefined Christianity and democratized religious expression, showing how faith can be both resilient and transformative.

The catalysts for the evolution of believe are varied, with technological advancements and globalization serving as key drivers of change. Innovations in technology challenge traditional beliefs, inviting us to rethink how we experience and express spirituality. From online worship platforms to digital prayer tools, technology offers new ways to connect with the divine, transforming the spiritual landscape. This shift to digital spaces, as noted in current research, not only alters the way we practice spirituality but also impacts the accessibility and inclusivity of spiritual experiences. Globalization, too, broadens our perspectives, exposing us to diverse beliefs and practices that enrich our understanding of faith. The exchange of ideas across cultures fosters a more inclusive and interconnected spiritual community.

Embracing the evolution of faith requires openness and adaptability. Engaging with diverse communities is one way to expand our perspectives and deepen our understanding. Dialogue with others who hold different beliefs encourages empathy and mutual respect, enriching our spiritual journey. Continuous learning is also vital, as it keeps us informed about cultural and theological developments that shape the spiritual landscape. Staying curious and open to new ideas allows us to navigate the ever-changing terrain of faith with grace and resilience. By embracing change, we can cultivate a faith that is both rooted in tradition and responsive to the present, a faith that evolves with us as we grow.

Reflection Exercise: Embracing Faith Evolution

1. Identify Influences: Reflect on the life stages and cultural shifts that have shaped your beliefs. Consider how these influences have evolved over time.
7. Explore New Perspectives: Engage with diverse communities or participate in interfaith dialogues. Take note of how these experiences impact your understanding of faith.

8. Commit to Continuous Learning: Stay informed about cultural and theological developments. Read books, attend lectures, or engage in discussions that challenge and expand your perspectives.

By embracing the natural evolution of beliefs, we open ourselves to a richer, more profound spiritual experience, one that reflects the complexities and beauty of life itself.

10.1 Envisioning a Personal Spiritual Future: Setting Intentions

Imagine standing at the edge of a vast, open field, the horizon stretching endlessly before you. This is your spiritual future, a landscape waiting to be shaped by your intentions and choices. Envisioning this future begins with setting clear intentions, guiding you toward a path that aligns with your deepest values and aspirations. Visualization exercises can be powerful tools in this process. Picture a life where your spiritual practices are seamlessly woven into your daily routine, where each action reflects your core beliefs. This mental imagery helps crystallize your goals, making them more tangible and achievable.

Setting intentions is not just about dreaming; it's about creating a roadmap for your spiritual aspirations. Goal-setting frameworks can transform these dreams into actionable steps, providing structure and direction. Begin by identifying your spiritual priorities, those aspects of life that resonate most profoundly with you. Perhaps it's cultivating mindfulness, deepening your connection with nature, or engaging more fully in community service. Once these priorities are clear, break them down into specific, achievable goals. This might involve dedicating time each day to meditation, volunteering for a cause you care about, or learning about different spiritual traditions. Each step, no matter how small, brings you closer to the spiritual life you envision.

The role of intention in spiritual growth cannot be overstated. Setting clear intentions directs your energy toward meaningful growth, focusing your efforts and resources on what truly matters. It's like a compass, providing direction when you feel lost or uncertain. Aligning your actions with these intentions ensures consistency in your spiritual practice, reinforcing your commitment to your goals. This alignment creates harmony between your inner values and outward actions, fostering a sense of integrity and authenticity. Through this process, you build a life that reflects your true self, where each decision is a step toward the future you desire.

To help you stay committed to your spiritual goals, consider using practical tools that keep your intentions front and center. Creating a vision board can be a powerful visual reminder of your aspirations. Fill it with images, quotes, and symbols that represent your spiritual goals, placing it somewhere you will see it daily. This constant visual cue reinforces your commitment, keeping your intentions alive and vibrant. Regular reflection sessions are also valuable, offering opportunities to review your progress and adjust your intentions as needed. Set aside time each month to assess where you are, celebrate your achievements, and recalibrate your goals if necessary. This ongoing reflection ensures that your spiritual journey remains dynamic and responsive to your evolving needs.

Consider the story of a seeker who found fulfillment through intentional meditation practice. Struggling with anxiety, they set an intention to cultivate peace and presence in their daily life. By committing to a simple meditation routine each morning, they gradually experienced a profound transformation. The practice became a cornerstone of their spiritual life, providing clarity and calm amidst the chaos. Another example is a community member who achieved peace by aligning their daily actions with spiritual goals. They integrated simple acts of kindness and gratitude into their routine, fostering a deep sense of connection and purpose. These stories illustrate the power of intention to guide transformative journeys, offering hope and inspiration for your own path.

As you envision your spiritual future, remember that intentions are seeds planted in the fertile soil of your soul. With care and commitment, they will grow, shaping a life rich with meaning and fulfillment. The future is yours to create, one intention at a time.

10.2 The Role of Faith in a Changing World: Adapting to New Realities

Faith, like a river, flows and adapts to the landscape it traverses, but it can also change that landscape. In today's world, this landscape is marked by rapid change, presenting both challenges and opportunities for spiritual growth. One of the most pressing issues of our time is climate change, and faith communities are increasingly stepping up to address this global challenge. Many religious groups advocate for environmental stewardship, drawing on teachings that emphasize care for creation. Churches, synagogues, mosques, and temples worldwide are joining forces to promote sustainable practices, integrating spiritual values with ecological action. These faith-based responses to climate change highlight a powerful synergy between spirituality and environmentalism, underscoring the moral imperative to protect our planet for future generations.

The intersection of faith and technology presents another arena where adaptation is crucial. Digital innovations have transformed how we experience and practice spirituality, offering new ways to connect with the divine. Online worship services and virtual prayer circles have become commonplace, allowing individuals to participate from anywhere in the world. This shift to digital spaces broadens access, enabling those who might otherwise be isolated to engage with their spiritual communities. However, it also poses challenges, as the authenticity of spiritual experiences may be questioned when mediated through screens. Faith communities must navigate these digital innovations thoughtfully, balancing the benefits of connectivity with the need for genuine, embodied experiences.

Faith also plays a vital role in promoting social justice, offering a moral framework for addressing societal issues. Religious and spiritual communities have long been advocates for change, using their influence to support marginalized groups and promote equality. Interfaith coalitions are increasingly working together to combat racial inequality, recognizing that unity across religious lines strengthens their impact. These coalitions organize events, dialogues, and campaigns that raise awareness and foster solidarity, drawing on shared values of justice and compassion. Faith-led initiatives also extend to supporting marginalized communities, providing resources, advocacy, and refuge for those in need. From homeless shelters to food banks, these efforts demonstrate the tangible impact of faith in action, offering hope and support to the vulnerable.

Yet, the rapidly changing world presents challenges that faith communities must address to remain relevant. Secularization trends pose a significant challenge, as traditional religious practices often struggle to resonate with modern sensibilities. Balancing tradition with contemporary values requires innovation and openness, inviting new interpretations of age-old teachings. Faith leaders must engage with the world around them, addressing the ethical dilemmas that arise in complex moral landscapes. These dilemmas might include debates over bioethics, technological advancements, or social issues, requiring thoughtful and nuanced responses that reflect both spiritual wisdom and current realities.

Examples of adaptation in faith communities abound, illustrating the creativity and resilience of spiritual practices. Some churches have embraced online worship to reach a global audience, using technology to expand their reach and inclusivity. These virtual gatherings allow for diverse participation, fostering a sense of belonging even across great distances. In other cases, spiritual leaders advocate for inclusive policies within their traditions, recognizing the need to evolve in response to social change. By embracing diversity and championing inclusivity, these leaders ensure that their communities remain vibrant and relevant, resonating with their members' diverse needs.

Faith remains a guiding light in this world of constant flux, offering stability amidst uncertainty. It calls us to adapt, to find new ways to express and live our beliefs while remaining rooted in timeless values. As we navigate this changing world, faith invites us to engage with the challenges and opportunities before us, to act with courage and compassion, and to envision a future where spiritual and worldly concerns are harmoniously intertwined.

10.3 Embracing Mystery: The Beauty of Unanswered Questions

One of the most profound aspects of faith is its embrace of mystery. There is a unique allure in the unknown, a sense of beauty that arises when we accept that not everything can be fully understood or explained. Learning to find wonder in uncertainty can be liberating and enriching in a world that often seeks quick and definitive answers. It invites us to approach life with curiosity, allowing unanswered questions to be stepping stones rather than stumbling blocks. This perspective encourages us to view life as a tapestry of experiences woven together by the threads of mystery and discovery. The unknown becomes a canvas on which we paint our spiritual journey, each question adding depth and color to the picture.

Embracing mystery challenges the desire for certainty, urging us to recognize the limitations of seeking definitive answers. While certainty can provide comfort, it can also lead to dogmatism and rigid adherence to beliefs that stifle growth and exploration. We create space for curiosity and deeper inquiry by allowing questions to remain open. This openness transforms our spiritual exploration into a dynamic process, where each moment of doubt becomes an invitation to delve deeper into understanding. In letting go of the need for complete certainty, we cultivate a mindset that welcomes ambiguity, seeing it as an opportunity for growth rather than a threat. This approach aligns with the teachings of many spiritual traditions, which emphasize the value of humility and the recognition that human understanding is inherently limited.

To cultivate a mindset open to mystery, we can turn to practices that ground us in the present and foster acceptance. Mindfulness, with its focus on awareness and presence, encourages us to embrace each moment as it is without the need for full comprehension. By practicing mindfulness, we learn to sit with uncertainty, allowing it to be part of our experience rather than something to be resolved. Journaling can also be a powerful tool, providing a space to explore our reactions to uncertainty and reflect on the insights that arise from it. Through writing, we can articulate our thoughts and feelings, uncovering patterns and gaining clarity amidst the unknown. These practices empower us to approach mystery with grace and curiosity, embracing it as an integral part of our spiritual journey.

Consider the story of a philosopher who found peace in accepting life's mysteries. Initially driven by a quest for definitive answers, he realized that true wisdom lay not in knowing everything but in appreciating the wonder of the unknown. By embracing uncertainty, he discovered a deeper sense of connection and tranquility, as if the very act of letting go opened new pathways of understanding. Similarly, an artist drew inspiration from the enigmatic aspects of spirituality, finding that the unknown fueled creativity and expression. In the absence of clear boundaries, her art flourished, capturing the essence of life's mysteries in vibrant colors and bold strokes. These narratives illustrate how embracing mystery can lead to personal growth and fulfillment, offering a path to deeper connection and insight.

As we embrace the mystery inherent in faith, we acknowledge that not all questions have answers and that this is a source of beauty, not limitation. Mystery invites us to explore with open hearts and minds, to find strength in uncertainty, and to celebrate the wonder of the unknown. In doing so, we cultivate a rich and vibrant spiritual life, one that is ever-evolving and deeply connected to the mysteries of existence. As we conclude this chapter, let us hold space for the unanswered questions, recognizing their role in shaping our understanding and guiding us toward new horizons.

FAITH OR SELF-HELP?

In writing this book, as well as in integrating wellness practices into my life, I have found that faith and meditation share several intriguing similarities, especially regarding their effects on the mind, body, and spirit. Here are a few key parallels:

1. **Inner Calm and Centering:** Both faith and meditation provide a sense of inner peace and stability. Faith often brings comfort through believing in something greater than oneself, while meditation cultivates calmness by fostering a deep awareness of the present moment. Both practices can serve as a refuge from stress and anxiety.

2. **Focus and Intentionality: Meditation involves focused attention, whether on** breathing, a mantra, or simply observing one's thoughts. Faith also requires a focused intention, particularly in practices like prayer or devotion, where individuals direct their attention toward their beliefs, whether through ritual, song, or words. This intentional focus can help people connect with something beyond themselves.

3. **Self-Reflection and Personal Growth:** Faith and meditation often encourage introspection. In meditation, self-reflection occurs as one observes thoughts and emotions nonjudgmentally. Faith may prompt personal reflection on one's actions, values, and life path, encouraging growth in alignment with one's beliefs. Both practices can reveal more profound insights into oneself and cultivate a sense of purpose.

4. **Connection to Something Greater**: Both faith and meditation are tools for connection—faith connects people to their spiritual beliefs or to a divine presence. In contrast, meditation often fosters a feeling of connectedness to the universe or a higher consciousness. This sense of connection can create feelings of peace, compassion, and even humility.

5. **Emotional and Physical Well-Being:** Many studies show that faith and meditation positively affect mental and physical health. Faith can lead to a greater sense of hope, purpose, and resilience, while meditation has been shown to reduce stress, improve focus, and even lower blood pressure. The regular practice of either can lead to overall better well-being.

6. **Consistency and Discipline:** Both faith and meditation often require a level of commitment and discipline. Faith is maintained and strengthened through regular practices like prayer, attending services, or studying sacred texts. Similarly, meditation becomes more effective with regular practice. This discipline can help people feel more grounded, resilient, and connected.

In essence, both faith and meditation offer a path to greater self-awareness, resilience, and connection with something larger than oneself, and each can provide powerful resources for navigating life's challenges.

I must also speak about mindfulness in this recipe.

Mindfulness fits seamlessly into the narrative connecting faith and meditation, as it shares many of the same benefits and qualities. Here's how mindfulness complements and deepens these practices:

7. **Heightened Awareness and Presence:** Like meditation, mindfulness is about staying present and observing each moment fully. In faith practices, mindfulness can deepen one's connection by encouraging full presence during prayer, rituals, or devotion. This heightened awareness fosters a more genuine experience, making practitioners feel more connected to their beliefs and actions.

8. **Non-Judgmental Reflection:** Mindfulness emphasizes observing thoughts, feelings, and sensations without judgment—much like meditation. In faith contexts, this non-judgmental approach can lead to more compassionate self-reflection. It allows people to observe their thoughts and feelings with kindness, helping them align more deeply with

their values without harsh self-criticism. This opens the door to genuine personal growth and forgiveness.

9. **Stress Reduction and Emotional Resilience**: Mindfulness, faith, and meditation all contribute to stress reduction and improved resilience. By practicing mindfulness, individuals learn to notice stress triggers without reacting impulsively, which can lead to calmer, more centered responses. When combined with faith, this approach provides emotional support and a sense of surrender, helping individuals manage life's difficulties with resilience and calm.

10. **Cultivating Compassion and Gratitude**: Both mindfulness and faith encourage compassion and gratitude. Mindfulness encourages an open-hearted perspective, seeing each moment as worthy of attention and appreciation. This aligns well with faith traditions, often teaching gratitude and compassion as core values. Together, these practices encourage not only self-compassion but also kindness toward others.

11. **Path to Inner Peace and Fulfillment**: While meditation helps clear the mind and faith provides spiritual grounding, mindfulness combines both by promoting an ongoing state of inner peace and acceptance. Faith can deepen this by giving meaning and direction, while mindfulness brings clarity and peace in each moment, reducing the mental clutter that often disrupts one's sense of fulfillment.

12. **Accessible, Daily Practice**: Mindfulness is often seen as a bridge between formal meditation and everyday life. It doesn't require a specific ritual or setting, making it adaptable to daily routines. This makes it easy to integrate into both faith practices and secular meditation, transforming ordinary activities—eating, walking, listening—into moments of presence and connection.

Ultimately, mindfulness weaves into faith and meditation by bringing a grounded, moment-to-moment awareness that makes both practices more vibrant and immediate. It enhances one's experience of spirituality, self-reflection, and personal growth, allowing each moment to become an opportunity for connection, compassion, and inner peace.

CONCLUSION

As we conclude this journey through faith and doubt, I invite you to reflect on the path we've traveled together. We've navigated the intricate and often challenging terrain of spiritual exploration, examining the emotional highs and lows, the intellectual challenges, and the life-changing potential inherent in questioning and reevaluating beliefs. This journey has been about more than just navigating uncertainty; it's been about embracing the growth that comes from it.

Throughout the book, we have explored how doubt, rather than being an obstacle, can serve as a catalyst for deeper understanding and personal development. We've examined the dynamic nature of faith, acknowledging that it is not static but rather evolves with our life experiences, cultural contexts, and individual reflections. This evolution is a testament to the strength and resilience inherent in the human spirit.

As you think back on the central themes we've discussed, remember the power of doubt as a transformative force. Doubt encourages us to question, to explore, and to seek out new perspectives. It has the potential to deepen our faith, making it more robust and reflective of our true selves. The journey of faith is not a straight line but a winding path full of unexpected turns and discoveries.

One of the key takeaways I hope you carry forward is the importance of embracing both certainty and uncertainty, recognizing that they are two sides of the same coin. Let doubt be a companion on your journey, guiding you toward a more profound and meaningful spirituality. Remember the strategies and practices we've explored, from mindfulness and journaling to engaging in open dialogues and seeking reliable guidance. These are tools you can use to navigate your own faith journey, finding clarity and peace amidst the chaos.

I encourage you to apply what you've learned. Whether it's setting aside time for reflection, participating in community dialogues, or seeking out new experiences, let your actions be guided by the insights you've gained. Your spiritual journey is ongoing, and each step you take is an opportunity to learn, grow, and connect with the world around you.

As you continue on this path, I want to leave you with a message of hope and possibility. Your spiritual journey is a beautiful adventure, one that is filled with potential and discovery. Embrace the unknown with curiosity and courage, for it is in these moments of uncertainty that we often find the greatest strength. Vulnerability, rather than being a weakness, is a source of profound connection and understanding. It allows us to be open to new experiences and perspectives, enriching our spiritual lives in ways we might never have imagined.

I am deeply grateful to you for joining me on this exploration of faith and doubt. Your willingness to question, to seek, and to grow is a testament to your courage and resilience. As you move forward, may you continue to embrace the complexities and joys of your unique spiritual path. May you find comfort in the questions, strength in the doubts, and joy in the discoveries. Let this journey be a reminder that you are never alone and that the pursuit of understanding is a shared endeavor, one that binds us all in our search for meaning and connection.

Thank you for being a part of this journey. Keep seeking, keep questioning, and keep growing. Your spiritual adventure awaits, and it is one filled with endless possibilities.

REFERENCES

- Jung on Belief, Doubt and Trust https://jungiancenter.org/jung-on-belief-doubt-and-trust/

- The Stages of Faith According to James W. Fowler | https://www.institute4learning.com/2020/06/12/the-stages-of-faith-according-to-james-w-fowler/

- Descartes' Epistemology - Stanford Encyclopedia of Philosophy https://plato.stanford.edu/entries/descartes-epistemology/

- The Enlightenment's Criticism of Religion: Theology https://academic.oup.com/book/38895/chapter/338046901#:~:text=While%20the%20Enlightenment%20is%20often,conception%20of%20God%20and%20immortality.

- Rebuilding Personal Identity During a Faith Transition https://www.psychologytoday.com/us/blog/leadership-diversity-and-wellness/202406/rebuilding-personal-identity-during-a-faith

- In a Crisis, Spiritual Resilience Can Pull Us Through https://www.authoracare.org/in-a-crisis-spiritual-resilience-can-pull-us-through

- Shame on You: The Challenge of Religious Guilt https://psychcentral.com/blog/blog/2018/05/shame-on-you-the-challenge-of-religious-guilt

- 5 Tips for Building True Spiritual Community https://www.churchleadership.com/leading-ideas/5-tips-for-building-true-spiritual-community/

- Leaving Religion: Nones, religious share stories of their faith https://www.northjersey.com/story/life/2021/10/03/leaving-religion-nones-share-stories/5924855001/

- Exploring Faith Transition Through the Lens of Cognitive ...
  https://wasatchfamilytherapy.com/blog/faith-transition-cognitive-dissonance

- 7 Hopeful Interfaith Stories from the Last Decade
  https://www.linkedin.com/pulse/7-hopeful-interfaith-stories-from-last-decade-raushenbush

- The Influence of the Secular Humanist Worldview
  https://www.summit.org/resources/articles/the-influence-of-the-secular-humanist-worldview/

- Cognitive Dissonance and Its Effects on Religious Beliefs
  https://digitalcommons.liberty.edu/cgi/viewcontent.cgi?article=1186&context=honors

- Creation vs. Evolution: Paradigms - Faith & Science ...
  https://discourse.biologos.org/t/creation-vs-evolution-paradigms/45349

- Christian existentialism
  https://en.wikipedia.org/wiki/Christian_existentialism

- "God is dead": What Nietzsche really meant
  https://bigthink.com/thinking/what-nietzsche-really-meant-by-god-is-dead/

- 33 Spirituality Journal Prompts to Connect to Your Spirit
  https://zannakeithley.com/spirituality-journal-prompts/

- Mindfulness Techniques for Self-Doubt in Coaching
  https://www.linkedin.com/advice/1/coaching-client-self-doubt-challenges-how-can-bqabf

- The Power of Open Discussion: Insights from the Bible
  https://digitalbible.ca/article-page/modern-topics-what-does-the-bible-say-about-open-discussion

- How To Find A Spiritual Mentor | Finding A True Guru
  https://nurtureyourspirit.org/how-to-find-a-spiritual-mentor/

- Toward a Conceptualization of Spiritual Identity Development
  https://scholarsarchive.byu.edu/cgi/viewcontent.cgi?article=3048&context=facpub#:~:text=This%20sense%20of%20spiritual%20identity,Richards%20%26%20Bergin%2C%201997).

- Sacred Spaces, Healing Places: Therapeutic Landscapes ...
  https://www.ncbi.nlm.nih.gov/pmc/articles/PMC4352605/

- Exploring the trend in religious diversity: Based on ...
  https://www.ncbi.nlm.nih.gov/pmc/articles/PMC9282533/

- The Importance of Spiritual Flexibility
  https://cslnashville.org/prayer-treatments/f/the-importance-of-spiritual-flexibility

- Feminist Theology
  https://www.thegospelcoalition.org/essay/feminist-theology/

- Navigating LGBTQ+ Identities & Religion
  https://www.thetrevorproject.org/resources/article/navigating-lgbtq-identities-and-religion/

- The Role of Technology in Modern Church Leadership
  https://pastorresources.com/transforming-worship-with-technology/

- Faith \u0026 The Environment
  https://www.earthday.org/campaign/faith-the-environment/

- Compassionate Listening: What Is It?
  https://www.patheos.com/articles/compassionate-listening

- Building Unity: Powerful Interfaith Dialogue Examples - Tazkiyah https://kharchoufa.com/en/interfaith-dialogue-examples/

- The Power of Story to Shape Our Faith https://janellrardon.com/2023/07/the-power-of-story-to-shape-our-faith/

- from religious diversity to spiritual inclusion https://diversiton.com/spiritual-inclusion/

- How to Welcome Criticism and Respond to It with Grace https://www.epm.org/resources/2021/Aug/23/welcome-criticism-respond-grace/

- Success 2.0: The Psychology of Self-Doubt https://hiddenbrain.org/podcast/the-psychology-of-self-doubt/

- The Power of Vulnerability: How Embracing It Can ... https://medium.com/a-smiling-world/the-power-of-vulnerability-how-embracing-it-can-supercharge-personal-growth-94319affa8f8

- The Mindset Shift: Transforming Fear into Courage https://medium.com/@timcastle_/the-mindset-shift-transforming-fear-into-courage-978a4998e795

- Surviving a Crisis of Faith https://www.boundless.org/faith/surviving-a-crisis-of-faith/

- Watkins' Spiritual 100 List for 2023 https://www.watkinsmagazine.com/watkins-spiritual-100-list-for-2023

- 100+ Spiritual Affirmations to Awaken Your Soul https://blog.gratefulness.me/spiritual-affirmations/

- Gratitude as a spiritual discipline https://www.umcjustice.org/latest/gratitude-as-a-spiritual-discipline-1201

- Establishing Daily Personal Spiritual Practices https://thedruidsgarden.com/2020/09/27/daily-rituals-and-daily-spiritual-practices/

- The Psychological and Spiritual Dimension of Volunteering https://www.researchgate.net/publication/370188175_The_Psychological_and_Spiritual_Dimension_of_Volunteering

- Interfaith Dialogue as Co-Creative Process https://learn.elca.org/jle/interfaith-dialogue-as-co-creative-process/

- How To: Integrate Your Faith with Your Career https://www.okwu.edu/tower-articles/how-to-integrate-your-faith-with-your-career/

- Hunter-Gatherers and the Origins of Religion - PMC https://www.ncbi.nlm.nih.gov/pmc/articles/PMC4958132/

- Renewing human spirituality in a technology-driven world? https://www.sciencedirect.com/science/article/abs/pii/S0747563223002558

- Bridging Faith and Social Justice Across Generations https://ssir.org/articles/entry/bridging_faith_and_social_justice_across_generations

- Embracing Mystery | Spiritual Practices for Everyday Life https://www.spiritualityandpractice.com/practices/features/view/17863?id=17863